HOOPS!

HOOPS!

The Official National Basketball Players Association Guide to Playing Basketball

•

GIORGIO GANDOLFI
AND
GERALD SECOR COUZENS

Photos by Giorgio Gandolfi

McGraw-Hill Book Company

New York   St. Louis   San Francisco
Bogotá   Guatemala   Hamburg   Lisbon
Madrid   Mexico   Montreal   Panama
Paris   San Juan   São Paulo   Tokyo   Toronto

PHOTO CREDITS:

page 12: Steve Toporov

pages 44 and 59: Andrew Bernstein

page 95: Courtesy of Phoenix Suns

page 98: Courtesy of Cleveland Cavaliers

page 118: Courtesy of Houston Rockets

page 143: Courtesy of Utah Jazz

page 174: Courtesy of Seattle Supersonics

page 175: Courtesy of Dallas Mavericks

6 7 8 9   SEM SEM

ISBN 0-07-013276-3

LIBRARY OF CONGRESS CATALOGING-IN-PUBLICATION DATA

Gandolfi, Giorgio.
    Hoops!: the official National Basketball Players
Association guide to playing basketball.
    1. Basketball.   I. Couzens, Gerald Secor.
II. National Basketball Players Association.
II. Title
GV885.G27 1987   796.32′3   86-7447

Designed by *Paul Chevannes*

FOREWORD

The players of the National Basketball Association are the best basketball players and some of the most talented athletes in the world. They got where they are today not only through talent, hard work, and dedication to their sport, but also because they are able to execute the basic fundamentals of the game consistently. On the court an NBA player makes his offensive moves so smoothly that they appear almost effortless. But observe closely and you'll see that every step, every pass and dribble has meaning to it. There's little wasted motion at this level of the game.

Fans and weekend players, as well as high school and college players alike, marvel at the immense skill of the pro players and want to know just how they do what they do on the court. Wherever they go, NBA players are constantly stopped and asked advice and guidance on all aspects of the game: How do you shoot a jump shot? What's the best way to get position for an offensive rebound? What are the best ball-handling drills to practice?

No pro player can ever give you a secret formula which will tell you how to become a good offensive basketball player. Such a formula doesn't exist. But they can tell you how to perform the fundamentals correctly. That's what this book is all about.

Every basketball player wants to be able to develop and utilize all of his basketball talent. Every coach wants the same for his players, too. This book provides recommended guidelines that both players and coaches can follow to become better at basketball. For the first time ever, the NBA's top players have collected their drills, favorite moves, and insights about the offensive game. Included here are all the "how-to's," advice from the best players on proper dribbling, passing, shooting, moving without the ball, and rebounding. Follow along and you'll learn step-by-step from the game's top players just how they execute various moves and why.

Presented here in ten chapters is a comprehensive look at the individual offensive game. Use this book as a stepping stone, a solid basis to help you get off on the right foot. If there is a strong enough will then you will succeed in basketball. With this book we certainly have provided you with the way to succeed. It's now up to you.

—JUNIOR BRIDGEMAN, *President*
National Basketball Players Association

AUTHOR'S NOTE

Solely in the interest of readability and sentence structure we have chosen to write this book in the masculine gender. Each year, the number of high school and university basketball competitions for girls and women is increasing, as is the pool of talent. In international competition American women basketball players lead the way. We salute these girls and women for the great strides they have made in the last decade, and hope that they, together with our male readers, will benefit from this book.

ACKNOWLEDGMENTS

This book involved the efforts of many individuals, and we would like to thank everyone who gave us both their time and insight and helped make this book possible.

Awakened from naps, grabbed before games, in hotel lobbies, on the team bus, in the locker room, and at home, the NBA players contributed ungrudgingly, happy to describe exactly the best way to make particular offensive moves. For this we are grateful.

Special thanks also goes to each team public-relations director and NBA player representative. It was a joint effort in helping us track down players for our little "talks"; to Larry Fleisher and Charles Grantham of the Players Association, and to Curtis, who always came up with the guarded phone numbers when needed; and to Jim "Hondo" Trupin, who orchestrated the game, hit the long shots, and mixed it up underneath when called upon. Keep smiling!

Getting out the final copy is a monumental task. Leslie Meredith and Lisa Frost, our editors and hoop fans, are responsible for this. Thanks for making a difficult task a pleasure.

GIORGIO GANDOLFI
GERALD SECOR COUZENS

CONTENTS

HOOPS!

CHAPTER 1

PHYSICAL CONDITIONING: OFF-SEASON TRAINING FOR BASKETBALL

How to Increase Power, Strength, Speed, Coordination, and Agility

WITH GARY VITTI

Gary Vitti received his MS in Sports Medicine from the University of Utah in 1982. He served as an instructor at the University of Utah and soon after designed and implemented a new curriculum program in sports medicine at the University of Portland. He joined the Los Angeles Lakers as chief trainer in 1984.

On a purely physical level, basketball is perhaps the most demanding of all sports. It's a game of quickness: fast starts, sharp cuts and turns, acceleration and deceleration, and, of course, jumping. The heart of the game is running, and plenty of it. In a 48-minute NBA game it's estimated that a starting player will have to run the 94-by-50-foot floor for a total of between four to six miles. This running includes sprinting up and down court on fast breaks, as well as chasing players cross-court, breaking through picks, and scampering behind a series of screens to get a shot off.

An NBA player has to be able to perform at high talent levels night after night throughout the eight-month-long, 82-game season. He can do this because he has prepared himself in the off-season by working out, putting into practice training princi-

1

ples that will help maintain his fitness at a high level and therefore bring out the most of his athletic potential.

Off-season training for competitive basketball at any level requires self-discipline, dedication, and sacrifice as well as knowledge of athletic training principles. Many talented young people never reach their full potential because they simply don't know what to do to achieve and maximize their basketball ability.

In past years it was generally accepted that the preseason training camp was the best time to condition yourself for the upcoming competitive season. This isn't true any more. Today, if a player doesn't come to an NBA preseason camp in optimum physical shape, he may injure himself, drop down a few spots on the roster, or get traded. Training camp is a time for fine-tuning parts of your game and to plan on team strategy. It's not a time to get into playing shape.

It is for this reason that the off-season is used to follow a training program to develop endurance, strength, speed, coordination, and agility. In order to be successful, all off-season training programs should include the following:

1. Warm-up of 5 to 10 minutes to increase blood flow and lubricate the joints.

2. Flexibility exercises to slowly stretch muscles and tendons that cross and surround your joints.

3. Strength development to increase muscular power and force.

4. Endurance or aerobic work to increase and maintain a high level of cardiovascular conditioning, and interval workouts to increase speed and stamina.

5. A cool-down period of 5 to 10 minutes after the exercise has finished to let the heart rate return to normal and facilitate the return of blood from the extremities.

6. Post-exercise flexibility exercises of 5 to 10 minutes to prevent muscles from shortening.

Warm-Up

WITH GARY VITTI

All exercise should be preceded by a short warm-up period of 5 to 10 minutes. The purpose of the warm-up is to prepare your body for more strenuous activity to follow. This program should consist of motions that simulate the actual exercises that are to be performed.

The warm-up routines will greatly increase the flow of blood to the muscle tissues and lubricate the joints, allowing you to bend, stretch, jump, and run to your maximum ability with little fear of injury. Exercise without a proper warm-up is very taxing to the muscles, tendons, ligaments, and joints of the body and may very easily lead to injury.

Warm-ups should be done with little or no resistance. Good warm-up exercises include skipping rope, jogging, riding a bike, or light calisthenics. Once you are lightly sweating, you are probably sufficiently warmed up (Fig. 1-1).

1-1. Kareem Abdul-Jabbar works regularly with the "HEAVYROPE"™ jump rope to increase his endurance and agility.

Flexibility

WITH GARY VITTI

Flexibility exercises should always follow your warm-up period. The reason for doing these exercises is to increase and therefore improve the range of motion of the joints that you will use in basketball. By increasing your range of motion, you will decrease your chance of injury during a basketball practice or game.

Flexibility for basketball can be achieved over a period of time by slow, passive stretching of the muscles and tendons that are used in basketball. Doing the exercises slowly is important in order to keep from injuring yourself by pushing the muscle too far, too fast.

Do not bounce as you stretch. This will cause the muscle to contract automatically, preventing it from reaching its maximum length. Continuous bouncing (ballistic stretching) can also cause a muscle to tear (Fig. 1-2).

Breathing and concentration are also very important in flexibility exercises. You should concentrate on the area being stretched and slow your breathing down in an

1-2. Akeem Olajuwon goes through a rigorous warm-up and stretching routine prior to playing.

attempt to relax that part of the body. Hold the stretch positions a minimum of 20 seconds and perform each stretch at least twice per session.

Basic Stretching Exercises for Basketball

WITH GARY VITTI

CALF

Stand a short distance from a wall. Keep your feet flat on the ground and place your forearms on the wall, your forehead leaning on the backs of your hands. Bend your left knee and bring it toward the wall. Keep the right leg straight. Begin to move your hips forward and this will start to stretch your right calf muscle. Hold this stretch for 20 seconds, straighten up, then repeat with the other leg. If you want to stretch the Achilles tendon, bend slightly at the knee and repeat the same routine.

GROIN

While sitting on the floor, join the soles of your feet together and hold them with your hands. Your elbows should be leaning on the insides of your legs. Lean your upper body forward by pushing with your hips. Once you feel mild tension in your groin, hold the stretch at that point for 20 seconds, then slowly sit up. Repeat.

HAMSTRINGS

Sit on the floor with legs crossed in front of you. Slowly straighten out your left leg, keeping the toes pointed straight up. Keep your right leg bent with the foot facing the inner part of your left leg. Lean forward from the hips until you begin to feel a mild form of discomfort in your hamstrings (the muscle on the back of your upper leg). Hold the stretch for 20 seconds and repeat with the other leg.

BACK

Lie on your back on the floor with both legs flat on the ground. Raise your right leg up, holding it just below the knee. Slowly bring it up toward your chest. Keep your head down on the floor and your left leg as straight as possible. Hold this stretch for 20 to 30 seconds. Lower your leg and repeat the exercise five times with each leg.

SHOULDERS

Pull your elbow across your chest and toward your opposite shoulder. With your opposite hand, slowly pull your elbow in the direction of the stretch. Hold for 20 seconds and repeat.

IMPORTANT STRETCHING POINTERS

- Stretching shouldn't be painful, but you should feel some mild tension or discomfort. Stop immediately once you feel sharp pain.

- Breathe naturally as you stretch. Don't hold your breath or you may pass out.

- Never bounce as you stretch. This will prevent you from properly stretching the muscle and could lead to injury.

- Stretching is an individual exercise. Don't compare your flexibility to that of a teammate. Some people are just more naturally flexible than others.

Stretching exercises for basketball will benefit everyone when done correctly. Remember, you only have to be flexible enough to play basketball. This doesn't mean that you have to stretch until you can perform a split or do a backward walkover. It's important to stress that the child athlete should never try for extreme flexibility. The musculoskeletal systems of children are not mature enough for too much stretching. Overstretching the joint tissues can result in long-term joint instability.

Strength Development

WITH GARY VITTI

By developing your physical strength over a period of time through weightlifting you will maximize and enhance your athletic skills. The basis of all strength training is progressive resistance. This means that as your body becomes accustomed to one particular weight over a period of time and you can perform an exercise with little strain, more weight is progressively added.

There are three basic forms of strength training. Isometric exercise is performed by contracting the muscles against a stationary, immovable object. An example of this is to stand in a doorway and extend arms, pushing against the doorjambs. Today, isometric exercise is mostly used in rehabilitation programs and is rarely used as a form of serious strength training for healthy athletes, because muscles cannot be strengthened by isometrics through their full range of motion.

Free-weight training is perhaps the most popular and common form of strength training. As you exercise with free weights (dumbbells and barbells) the muscles being worked meet the same amount of resistance throughout the complete range of motion that you decide to put them through. If you are bench-pressing 200 pounds, your muscles have 200 pounds of resistance in the beginning, middle, and end of the lift.

A distinct advantage that free weights have over weight machines, the other major form of strength training, is that free weights are just more versatile. With dumbbells, for example, you can move through a complete muscle range, thereby developing much greater overall strength. A 110-pound set of free weights costs about $90 and takes up less space than the much more costly weight machine.

A drawback to strength training with a machine is that if you are too tall or too small for the machine, you will never achieve good results because you simply won't fit properly on the machine. For serious sports training, most strength coaches are in agreement that it's free weights, supplemented with weight machines, that yield the best results.

Generally speaking, guards and small forwards should be concerned with adding muscle tone (i.e., using *less* weight and doing more reps), while the centers and power forwards should be concerned with building bulk (i.e., using *more* weight and doing fewer reps).

To design your own strength program, start by finding your single-lift capacity for each exercise. This is the maximum amount of weight you are able to comfortably lift one time using strictly correct lifting form. The program is derived from percentages of that single-lift capacity.

GUARDS AND SMALL FORWARDS

1. Amount of weight to be lifted: 60 to 70 percent of your single-lift capacity.

2. Number of repetitions per set: 10 to 15. (A set is a series of repetitions.)

3. Number of sets per lift: minimum of three.

4. Progressive weight increase: Increase poundage only when you can comfortably complete all three sets in strictly correct form.

POWER FORWARDS AND CENTERS

1. Amount of weight lifted: 70 to 80 percent of single-lift capacity.

2. Number of repetitions per set: 8 to 10.

3. Number of sets per lift: minimum of three.

4. Progressive weight increase: Increase poundage only when you can comfortably complete all three sets in strictly correct form.

The Los Angeles Lakers Strength Training Program

WITH GARY VITTI

The most efficient manner of strength training is to work the larger muscle groups first and then progress to the smaller muscle groups. For example, you should not do triceps exercises prior to the bench press, because the triceps get worked during the bench press as well. If they are fatigued, then you will be unable to load the chest muscles effectively in the bench press.

The strength program will consist of three-day-per-week total-body conditioning for guards and small forwards and a "split program" that is followed four days a week for centers and power forwards. Both programs can be done at home with your own free weights and a weightlifting bench, or else at a health club or school weight room with proper equipment.

Begin each lifting session with a 5-to-10-minute warm-up session consisting of light jogging, rope skipping, or stationary bike riding to get your heart rate elevated and your muscles warm. You should be breathing and sweating freely. Follow this up with your stretching routine to get the muscles to their maximum length.

If you don't know the proper way to do the following weightlifting exercises, consult a strength coach at a school or club to show you how to perform the exercises. Strict lifting form is essential in strength training; improper form will lead to injury or keep you from achieving maximum gains.

The body parts and exercises are listed as follows:

Chest	decline bench flys bench press incline bench		*Back*	bent over rows Universal lat pull Nautilus pullover
Shoulders	seated military press shoulder shrugs upright rows Nautilus double shoulder		*Arms*	curls with barbell or dumbbells Nautilus curls dips triceps extensions Nautilus tri extensions
Legs	leg extensions leg curls squats lunges hack			

To make use of the following chart (pages 10 and 11), simply record the weight you lifted for each set, as well as for each body part.

Consistency is a key element in the success of your weight training program. A record keeping system such as this one charts the weight you've lifted and serves as a handy reference of your progress. With this chart you'll be able to accurately note the effects of your program and make changes when needed.

Weights and Children

WITH GARY VITTI

An issue that has received a great deal of attention regarding strength training concerns the question of when and if a child athlete should begin weightlifting. The current feeling today is that weight training can be started in the high school years and not before. There is a twofold reason for this. Prior to this age young athletes don't possess the hormone level that will allow for significant gains in weight training. Secondly, the fact that the child is still in a growth state allows for the susceptibility of injury to the growth plates of the bones. If a child is interested in strength training, it is recommended that he participate in resistance training using his own body weight as the resistance—performing such exercises as push-ups, sit-ups, pull-ups, dips, and leg raises.

Endurance (Cardiovascular) Training

WITH GARY VITTI

Endurance training is important because it provides you with a sufficient fitness foundation to enable you to play a full-court game of basketball without being weakened by fatigue. Endurance or cardiovascular exercise is better known as aerobic training. Aerobic training is a method of developing the heart and lung tissues to make them work more efficiently. As you increase your aerobic capacity by running, cycling, or swimming, your cardiovascular system will be able to supply more oxygen to your working muscles with less effort than before. You are getting in shape and it will show on the basketball court (Fig. 1-3).

When you are aerobically fit, fatigue will not hit you until late in a game. And once you do get tired, after a brief rest you'll be able to recover quickly from your fatigue and continue to play at pretty much the same level of intensity as before.

To start your off-season aerobic training, choose an endurance exercise that is most comfortable and enjoyable for you. Exercise physiologists have found that the greatest improvements in aerobic capacity occur when you either cross-country ski, run, cycle, or swim at 70 percent of your maximum heart rate for at least 20 uninterrupted minutes

PROGRAM FOR GUARDS AND SMALL FORWARDS*

Body Part		Chest	Chest	Shoulder	Shoulder	Back	Back	Biceps	Triceps	Quads	Quads	Ham	Groin	Calf	Abdominal
Exercise	sets →														
Monday	1st														
	2nd														
	3rd														
Wednesday	1st														
	2nd														
	3rd														
Friday	1st														
	2nd														
	3rd														

* Choose the appropriate number of exercises per body part from the list on page 8. Perform these exercises at 60 to 70 percent of maximal lifting capacity—10 to 15 reps per set.

PROGRAM FOR POWER FORWARDS AND CENTERS*

Body Part	Chest	Chest	Chest	Biceps	Biceps	Triceps	Triceps	Abdominals
Exercise sets →								
Monday 1st								
2nd								
3rd								
Thursday 1st								
2nd								
3rd								

Body Part	Shoulder	Shoulder	Shoulder	Back	Back	Quads	Quads	Hams	Groin	Calf
Exercise sets →										
Tuesday 1st										
2nd										
3rd										
Friday 1st										
2nd										
3rd										

* Choose the appropriate number of exercises per body part from the list on page 8. Perform these exercises at 70 to 80 percent of maximal lifting capacity—8–10 reps per set.

11

1-3. The Philadelphia 76ers at their September preseason training camp are being timed for the mile run.

three to five times a week. All of these aerobic exercises are rhythmic in nature and use your large muscle groups (legs, chest, arms), developing and strengthening them with little stress to your musculoskeletal system (except from running).

Swimming is an excellent aerobic conditioner and relatively stress-free, but it does require access to a swimming pool on a regular basis as well as an ability to swim. Cross-country skiing is the best aerobic exercise there is because it works both the upper and lower body equally with no stress to your joints. Although it is a seasonal activity dependent on snowfall, there is now a home machine available which simulates the cross-country movements and will give you a very good workout. (This machine does cost several hundred dollars, however.)

Since you can run almost anywhere in all types of weather, at most any time of the day, distance running is by far the most popular form of aerobic training, and the one that the majority of pro basketball players take part in during the off-season. The only piece of equipment that you have to invest in is a quality pair of running shoes. Well-constructed running shoes will absorb the shock of three to five times your body weight that comes crashing down with each footfall as you run. If you neglect to buy good running shoes, at some point you will begin to feel pain or discomfort in your feet, knees, hips, or back.

TRAINING AND YOUR HEART

Whichever off-season aerobic exercise you choose for yourself, in order to have any positive effects the exercise should:

- last a minimum of 20 uninterrupted minutes.

- be performed a minimum of three days per week.

- be performed at an intensity level of at least 70 percent of your maximum heart rate.

Aerobic exercise develops your heart muscle. An athletic heart, one developed by following a regular exercise program, is larger, heavier, beats slower, and pumps blood more efficiently than an untrained heart.

Taking your pulse as you exercise in the off-season is a good way to monitor your current physical state as well as your level of exercise intensity. The easiest way to monitor your pulse is with a portable heart-rate monitor. There are many models now available. Expect to pay $140 to $300 for a quality monitor. The benefit of a pulse-rate monitor is that by simply glancing at the monitor you get a pulse reading without having to interrupt your workout to take your pulse.

The best way to take your pulse by hand is to use your three middle fingers and press them gently on the radial artery of your wrist, located just below the thumb. Count the beats (starting with zero) for six seconds and add a zero to the number that you've counted. Take your pulse in the morning just before getting out of bed and you'll have your *resting pulse rate*. Take it immediately following exercise and you'll have your *training heart rate*. Your heart rate is the best indicator of how hard you're exercising. Therefore, aerobic workouts are best monitored by keeping track of your heart rate.

In theory, you should exercise in a *target heart zone*. This is a pulse count that ranges from 60 percent all the way up to 85 percent of your maximum heart rate. Your maximum heart rate is the theoretical number of beats that your heart can pump per minute.

As you exercise, your heart rate increases to keep up with your body's demand for oxygen. The harder and longer you exercise, the higher your heart rate will be. To find your maximum heart rate, simply subtract your age from 220 if you are a man and from 226 if you are a woman. The number that you get is your current maximum heart rate. To find your target heart zone, the heartbeat range that you want to perform your exercise in, subtract your resting heart rate from your maximum heart rate and multiply this number by .60. Add your resting heart rate to this number and you'll come up with the low range of your target heart zone. To find the high range of it, follow the same procedure as above: subtract your resting heart rate from your maximum heart rate, multiply this number by .80, and add on your resting heart rate. Most trained basketball players will work out at 70 to 75 percent of their maximum heart rate, moving up to 85 percent or higher when they begin interval workouts.

Intervals

with Gary Vitti

One thing you should be aware of is that aerobic training at a long steady distance (LSD training) will lay the groundwork for a basketball fitness base, but it's interval training that will get you in shape to play a real fast-paced game. Intervals help you develop your explosiveness on the basketball court and are a key ingredient in helping you reach your potential as a basketball player.

An interval is a training method of alternating hard, short bursts of speed with short recovery periods of easier exercise. Intervals can be done running, cycling, swimming, rowing, or cross-country skiing. Intervals are important for basketball training because basketball is a fast-paced game of starts and stops and your energy output varies throughout the length of the game. Interval training duplicates this and helps to quickly raise your fitness to much higher levels.

If you were to limit your off-season training to distance running at a 7½-minute-mile pace, you might develop the endurance needed to last an entire basketball game, but you would never achieve the speed, strength, and power to keep up on fast breaks and in end-of-game situations where speed is still needed. It's only interval training that can dramatically increase your speed and stamina. If you leave intervals out of your off-season training, your physical condition will suffer.

The last three to four weeks of the off-season is the appropriate time to add intervals to your training program. Since intervals are very taxing to the body, they should never be done two days in a row; give your body at least 48 hours to recover between interval workouts. Also, before beginning any interval session, make sure that you are properly warmed up. Take the time to loosen up with stretching and you will help prevent any muscle injury. Once you begin your intervals, don't go all out on the first one, but try to target a level of intensity that you can maintain right through the last interval of the workout. You will gradually be able to increase the level of intensity of each workout.

SAMPLE INTERVAL RUNNING PROGRAM

Monday

1. 30-meter sprints: sprint one, walk back (5 times)

2. 50-meter sprints: sprint one, walk back (5 times)

3. 30-meter sprints: sprint one, walk back (3 times)

4. 50-meter sprints: sprint one, walk back (3 times)

Wednesday

1. 150 meters: sprint 50 meters, stride 50 meters, sprint 50 meters, walk back (8 times)

Friday

1. 30-meter sprints: sprint one, walk back (4 times)
2. 60-meter sprints: sprint one, walk back (4 times)
3. 100-meter sprints: sprint one, walk back (4 times)

Cool Down

WITH GARY VITTI

Any exercise period should be followed by a brief cool-down period of 5 to 10 minutes. Actually, the cool-down should be a continuation of the activity being performed, but done at a much lower level of intensity.

Post-Exercise Flexibility Exercises

WITH GARY VITTI

Flexibility exercises should always follow an exercise session. These flexibilities are done in the same manner as the pre-exercise stretching already described. Stretching after you work out will help stretch out muscles that have become tight and shortened because of the exercise.

Nutrition

WITH GARY VITTI

Several studies have pointed out that athletic performance is seriously hampered by inadequate nutrition. Hard training for basketball will quickly deplete your body of nutrients and energy. Proper nutritional habits are essential if you are going to keep up your training intensity. Eating a wide variety of foods from the four basic food groups assures you of a balanced diet containing all of the proper nutrients.

A balanced diet consists of foods from:

1. *Meat Group* (high in protein, vitamins, and minerals)

2. *Milk Group* (high in protein, fat, and calcium)

3. *Fruit and Vegetable Group* (high in carbohydrates, vitamins, and minerals)

4. *Bread and Cereal Group* (high in carbohydrates with some protein, vitamins, and minerals)

BASIC FOUR FOOD GROUPS

The foods from the four basic food groups should be divided into your diet as: 70 percent carbohydrates (principle energy source); 20 percent fat; and 10 percent protein. Competitive athletes should consume between 3,000 and 6,000 calories of food per day.

Thus, for example, a competitive basketball player eating 4,500 to 5,400 calories per day should consume:

Carbohydrates (70 percent)	3,150 calories
Fat (20 percent)	900–1,350 calories
Protein (10 percent)	450–900 calories
Total intake:	4,500–5,400 calories

GOOD SOURCES OF CARBOHYDRATES
(70% of Daily Caloric Intake)

breakfast cereals (unsweetened)
pasta
crackers (unsalted)
dried fruits
legumes
bananas
dates
white potatoes
   (without butter, sour cream, etc.)
sweet potatoes
liver

bread
rice
cornmeal
   (i.e., cornbread, corn muffins, etc.)
wheat
barley
buckwheat pancakes
cranberry sauce
skim milk
fruits
fruit juices

GOOD SOURCES OF FAT
(20% of Daily Caloric Intake)

vegetables
vegetable oils
   (i.e., fried foods)
vegetable shortenings
beef
lard

bacon
cheese
   (except cottage cheese)
potato chips
cakes
pastries

butter   candy
whole milk   whipped cream
eggs   sour cream
nuts   margarine
peanut butter   (better than butter, but not as tasty)
cookies   pies

GOOD SOURCES OF PROTEIN
(10% of Daily Caloric Intake)

soybeans   turkey
chicken   veal
fish

THE PREGAME MEAL

The pregame meal, that last meal that you take before going out to play your game, will have little effect on your physical performance. Rather, it's the meals that you've had during your training period that will provide you with the nutritional help needed to achieve your highest playing potential.

Essentially what a pregame meal does is minimize the sensation of hunger. This meal should be taken at least three to four hours before your game to allow for proper digestion and a relatively empty stomach when you play. You can choose from a wide variety of foods for your meal, but try to make sure that they are high in carbohydrates and low in proteins and sugar. A high-carbohydrate meal is good not only because it can be digested the fastest, but because the starches contained in the food are then stored in the muscles as glycogen, a body fuel that becomes readily available once you start to play basketball. Foods high in protein that are eaten less than three hours before you play are to be avoided because they contain fats that will stay too long in your stomach.

Here are some examples of nutritious pregame meals that can be taken before an afternoon or an evening game:

8-oz. glass of fat-free milk   8-oz. glass of fruit juice
2 poached eggs   vegetable soup
2 pieces of toast with jam   crackers
banana   low-fat cottage cheese

8-oz glass of orange juice
bowl of cereal without sugar
banana

The digestion time for a pregame meal composed chiefly of carbohydrates is about two hours; for a meal composed chiefly of protein, three hours; and for a meal laden with fats, it can be as long as five hours.

LIQUID MEALS

Commercially prepared liquid meals are very easily digested and contain a good balance of carbohydrates (a high percentage), fats, and proteins. The chief benefits of a liquid preparation are that the meal supplies all that the body needs and it will pass from the stomach very quickly. Also, because it is so easily digested, it can then be taken a lot closer to game time than a solid meal.

Drink Water

WITH GARY VITTI

Water plays the most important role in your athletic performance. By preventing excessive water loss while you play, you can maintain top form throughout the game.

It's a well-documented fact that excessive sweat lost during a workout or game is the major reason for sub-par performances. A way to prevent this is to keep hydrated by drinking plenty of water before, during, and after you play. A few hours before you are going to play it's important that you drink at least three glasses of water. Fifteen minutes before playing, drink another cup of water.

Once you start to play, a regular intake of water will help replace some of the water lost by sweating and will keep your muscles from overheating. It's a very good idea when playing to get into the habit of stopping regularly and drinking at least 10 ounces of water every 15 minutes.

Drink *before* you become thirsty. If you wait until you finally have the sensation of thirst, you may already have sweated off 1 percent or more of your body weight. This could mean two to five pounds of actual body weight that is lost.

Gulping down water at this time to replace what you've already lost and then going back to play will not have the immediate effect of improving your situation. Your body can't instantly absorb all of the water. Ten ounces of water at 15-minute increments seems to be the maximum that can be taken in. Drink more than this while you're playing and you may feel bloated and uncomfortable.

When you're playing basketball, what your body needs most is water, not sugared water. Contrary to the fancy advertising campaigns that show sweaty athletes chugging down frosty glasses of specially prepared "sport drinks," water is still the best fluid-replacement drink available. If you do decide to drink any of the commercially available "athletic" drinks, dilute them with two to three parts water. When taken undiluted, the high sugar content of these drinks can lead to a bloated feeling and possible stomach cramps.

When your workout is over you should drink plenty of water, your "sport drink," or fruit juice to replace lost body fluids. Proper fluid replacement will help prevent muscle cramping, a problem commonly linked with dehydration. If you like to drink beer, have just a few glasses. Drinking too much can lead to excessive urination, causing you to stay in a dehydrated state.

Prepare to Be a Winner

WITH GARY VITTI

A high level of personal motivation is critical to the success of anything that you do in life. No matter how much or how little actual basketball talent you have, if you are motivated enough to follow the preseason program that has been outlined here, you will get in shape and therefore be better able to achieve your goals.

All the many hours that you put into your conditioning program will eventually yield results. In the final minutes of a game when your team is desperately looking for someone to score, grab a rebound, or block a shot, it is you who will come through. Why? Because you are in shape and, even in the waning minutes when everyone else is tired, you can still perform at a high competitive level. With the base built from your preseason training program, you are the one who still has the mental toughness, the strength, the power, and the motivation to get the job done.

Although you may never have all of the tools to be the most talented basketball player, by working hard and following this preseason program, you will become a well-conditioned athlete, able to maximize all your basketball talents. In the end this will enable you to come as close as possible to achieving your basketball dreams.

CHAPTER 2

FUNDAMENTAL POSITION; BASIC MOVES WITHOUT THE BALL

Basketball Position

WITH JIM PAXSON
GUARD;   6'6",   200 LB.

Jim Paxson was the first-round draft choice of the Portland Trail Blazers after graduating from the University of Dayton in 1979, and ranks among Portland's all-time stat leaders. At the end of the 1985–86 season he had a 16.9-ppg career scoring average with well over 50 percent field goal accuracy. A member of the NBA All Star teams in 1983 and 1984, Paxson is the best in the NBA when it comes to moving without the ball.

Offensive basketball begins not with the basketball in your hands ready to take a shot, but with your fundamental position—how you actually stand on the court. Some coaches call this your "basketball position." Others refer to it as your "basketball stance" or "basketball posture." Whatever name it's given, it still comes down to the same fundamental position that you must hold: body kept low, knees flexed, feet kept apart at shoulders' width, hands raised at chest level and close to the body.

When a player is in this position he is balanced, able to receive the ball and move in any direction. When quick movements are needed, your basketball position keeps you set and ready to make them.

Basketball position is one of the least understood fundamentals of the game. Young players very often don't see or understand fully its relationship to shooting or scoring, facets of the game that they're generally more interested in. Unfortunately, they often neglect to work on their basketball position, or, worse yet, their coaches neglect to teach it. The "perfect" player, however, maintains his basketball position from the opening tip-off all the way through to the final buzzer.

Whenever I visit basketball camps I try to stress to campers the importance of proper body position on the court. I always tell them that not until they have this stance will they be able to move effectively and efficiently. If a player has good positioning, he's not only ready to receive the ball and then move with it on offense, but he can also make the quick transition over to defense when he has to. On the other hand, if a player is standing straight up with his hands on his hips, he's just not ready to make that split-second move. Correct positioning may not *seem* important but it's actually the *foundation* of your entire offensive and defensive game (Fig. 2-1).

FOOT PLACEMENT

Basketball is a game of quick moves, cuts, and pivots. To make any of these moves properly, you must start with good foot positioning. How and where your feet are positioned has a great effect on how the rest of your body moves and therefore on the quality of your game.

Keep your feet shoulders'-width apart, or even slightly further spread. The non-pivot foot should be slightly out in front of the other, with the toes of the pivot foot on the same plane with the heels of the front, or lead, foot. Either foot can be placed forward in this staggered stance. Choose the one which is more comfortable for you. Generally, right-handed players will lead with their right foot and pivot on their left; left-handed players lead with their left foot and pivot on their right.

Both feet should be flat on the floor, with your body weight distributed over the full length of each foot. A common mistake is to put full body weight only on the balls of the feet. This positioning fatigues the calf muscles and will also slow you down when you begin to make a move, because proper movement entails having the heels of the feet making contact with the floor.

LEG POSITION

Legs should always be flexed at the knee, so you are in a crouched position. This way you're able to react to any situation. When you keep the legs flexed, your muscles are "loaded," ready to give you needed power and quickness when you want it. When you stand straight-legged you lose this quickness, because your leg muscles are stretched out. Only when they first contract and then stretch out again will you be able to move with speed and power.

2-1. Jim Paxson has proper basketball position. His knees are flexed, his fingers spread wide, hands ready to receive the ball.

ARM POSITION

Keep your arms and hands held in close to your chest. The wrists and elbows must be flexed so you're able to receive the ball and help the body make quick moves. The fingers are kept spread out.

HEAD POSITION

How you hold your head will greatly affect your movement on the court. Holding your head too far backward or too far forward can knock your entire body out of balance. To be properly balanced, imagine a straight line running through the middle of your head, through your body, right to the floor to the space exactly between your two feet. Your head must sit right in the middle of this invisible line at all times. Remember: Your head is really the most important factor in body balance. If it's out of line, you'll never be able to achieve your full potential.

How to Move Quickly and Smoothly

WITH RICKEY GREEN
GUARD;   6'0",   170 LB.

Called "the fastest player on the court and maybe on ice too" by coach Frank Layden, Green holds the Utah Jazz career record for assists and steals. An All-American at the University of Michigan, he led his team to an NCAA championship runner-up finish in 1977. Green was co-captain of the 1984 West Team in the NBA All-Star game.

Basketball is a game of ever-changing tempos. In order to play the game effectively you have to be able to get from one spot on the court to another and to go from offense to defense as quickly and smoothly as possible. Quickness, rather than pure basketball talent, counts for a good portion of your success in the game. If you can hit your jumper consistently, then you will have a certain value to your team. But if you are slow— you're not able to get to different parts of the court very quickly—then your offensive skills will be of much less value when compared to those of a quicker teammate.

Speed and quickness, two important physical attributes needed to play basketball at a high level, are seemingly similar qualities, but they shouldn't be confused with each other. Your maximum level of speed—how fast you can actually run up and down the court—is a gift. It's an inherited characteristic that you can do nothing to change, but a lot to develop.

Although you can't alter your maximum speed, quickness on the basketball court is not an inherited trait and can be developed through practice. Even though you may not be the fastest "pure" runner, you can teach yourself to be quick. You can begin by always maintaining your basketball position and by diligently working on your starts, stops, pivots, and changes of pace. These are the seemingly simple yet little-practiced basketball movements that will help reduce and eliminate wasted body movement, streamline your moves, and make them more meaningful and efficient.

QUICK STARTS

Always do your best to maintain your basketball position. Throughout the game you must keep your legs slightly flexed, arms in, hands at chest level, and feet placed flat on the floor. Most importantly, be alert, ready to react and move.

When you make a movement to the right, start by turning your head in that direction while at the same time shifting your weight over your right foot as you move. It's extremely important for you to keep low. Pump with your arms to develop a powerful drive, and keep your initial steps short and fast. Quickness is enhanced by not taking long steps. How fast you can move your feet is much more important than how much distance you can cover with each stride.

Basic Movement without the Ball

WITH JUNIOR BRIDGEMAN
FORWARD/GUARD;   6'5",   215 LB.

Junior Bridgeman is rated as one of the NBA's top "sixth man." He is respected for his thorough knowledge of basketball fundamentals. Originally selected by the Los Angeles Lakers after his graduation from the University of Louisville in 1975, Junior Bridgeman was immediately traded to the Bucks where he played until 1985, setting a club record for games played. Bridgeman joined the Los Angeles Clippers in the 1984–85 season.

STOPS

Just as getting a quick start is important in basketball, equally important is being able to come to a quick stop and still be in a good basketball position, ready to play offense or defense. There are many instances in the course of a game when you'll get the ball on the run. Being able to stop immediately, then pivot, take a shot, or make a cut while maintaining your balance, will make you a dangerous offensive threat. But if you're off-balance when you stop, you then have to take the time to set yourself up, if only for an extra second. Unfortunately, this is just enough time to let the defensive player regain any advantage that you held over him.

There are two good ways of stopping on the court and it only takes a little practice to learn how to do both properly. After a few practice sessions these stops should become instinctive and part of your basketball repertoire.

THE QUICK (OR ONE-COUNT) STOP

This is perhaps the most basic stop in basketball. You make the quick stop off a run by landing with both feet on the floor at the same time, the heels touching first, your toes acting as brakes as they bend and flex to slow you down. Your knees are flexed, back bent slightly backward, head held horizontally. Your forward movement is effectively eliminated with this stop. By crouching as you land you're now in basketball position, ready to shoot, receive a pass, and make a cut (a sharp, quick move made to get open) in another direction.

THE STRIDE (OR TWO-COUNT) STOP

The stride stop is used when you are moving forward and need to change or reverse direction. It is also a good stop to use when you are dribbling and ready to go up for a jump shot. To perform the stride stop, land on your rear foot (this then becomes your pivot foot, so don't move it if you stop dribbling) and then your front foot. Keep your knees flexed and your back tilted slightly backward to slow your forward momentum.

PIVOTING

Pivoting, or turning, can be done with either your right or left foot. All that it entails is keeping one foot—your "pivot foot"—stationary, while you turn or spin your body around on the ball of your pivot foot. Pivoting can be done with or without the ball.

When you have the ball in your possession and have selected a foot to be your pivot foot, it must remain rooted to that spot on the floor. You will be called for a traveling violation if you decide to move the foot and begin to pivot with the other foot (Fig. 2-2).

In order to pivot properly, follow these simple rules:

• Keep your basketball position with legs flexed, feet shoulders'-width apart or wider.

- Pivots should be made on the ball of your foot. If you pivot on your heel, you'll lose your balance and possibly even trip.

- You can make a full 360-degree pivot or a half- or even a quarter-turn pivot. Just remember to keep your body low and your feet spread wide.

- It's best to make the pivot by swinging with your arm and elbow pointing in the new direction to help the body move quickly.

- Pivots are made offensively and defensively to the front or rear. A *front turn* is made when your chest moves around the pivot foot (a good way to square up to the basket for a shot), while a *rear turn* is made by leading first with your rear end.

- Pivots should be practiced on your right and your left foot to prepare you for possible game situations.

REVERSE

A reverse is simply a change-of-direction move made while you are running. Depending on your speed, use a one-count or two-count stop to make the move. Put your weight on your pivot foot, turn and make a quick step in the new direction with your new lead foot.

To make this a quick and smooth movement, as you pivot, point the foot of your new lead leg in the direction that you want to go. This will help you to maintain balance, but more importantly it will help your entire body to move in that new direction. Also, in pivoting, swing your arm and elbow to help quickly shift the weight of your body.

CHANGE OF PACE

Basketball is a game of ever-changing tempos and speeds and the change-of-pace movement is a good offensive move that should be used throughout the game.

The change of pace is a three-part move used to lose your defensive man. You execute it by running, then slowing down your pace and straightening up your body slightly to give the defense the impression that you are going to stop running. This will automatically relax the defense. If you bend over again and then quickly accelerate your pace, your defensive man will be knocked out of balance and won't be able to react quickly. You will now be in position to set up a play, receive the ball, or penetrate to the hoop with the ball.

Change of pace is an extremely important aspect of the game. You should use this move with or without the ball because basketball is a game of continuous fluctuations in speed. You cannot be successful by playing the game at only one speed.

2-2. Wayman Tisdale prepares to pivot to escape
two Knick defenders. The ball is well protected,
kept away from reaching hands.

2-3. Michael Jordan uses a change-of-direction move to cut and receive the ball. He pushes off strongly with his left foot as he heads to the right.

CHANGE OF DIRECTION

This is an explosive move that is used when you want to shake your defender, get free for a pass or possible shot, or just move to another part of the court. To change your direction as you run forward, place your outside foot down hard and put the weight of your body on this foot. This will help stop your forward movement. Quickly turn with your hips, trunk and head to the direction you want to go. Make sure that your forward foot is pointing straight. If, instead, you keep this foot pointed sideways, you'll never be able to generate enough power to help you push off explosively in the new direction (Fig. 2-3).

HOCKEY STEPS

As you are running forward at moderate speed, take a series of short, quick, parallel steps, staying low with your knees flexed. Combine this with a change-of-direction move and you'll have your defender scrambling behind you trying to catch up. Also, while you are making these steps, alternately shake your shoulders and head. This will confuse the defense because, with different parts of your body going in different directions, the defense can't be sure which way you will eventually run. This move is normally combined with a change of direction.

3-1. Moses Malone's intense determination helps him pull this offensive rebound between Robert Parish and Kevin McHale of the Boston Celtics.

OFFENSIVE REBOUNDING
Ingredients for Offensive Rebounding

WITH MOSES MALONE
CENTER; 6'10", 255 LB.

Malone, the NBA's Chairman of the Boards, led the league in rebounding in six of his nine pro seasons. His career high of 37 rebounds came against New Orleans on February 9, 1979. In the 1984–85 season Malone, nine-time All-Star selection, reached two milestones in his illustrious career, hitting the 15,000–NBA–point plateau and hauling in his 10,000th rebound.

Height and good jumping ability are certainly advantages in offensive rebounding, but they are by no means the only factors in becoming a good rebounder. There are some instances during the course of an NBA season when a seven-foot center is outbattled for a rebound, even outrebounded for an entire game, by a player as much as six inches shorter. Rebounding, the act of jumping up after missed shots, is an important basketball skill that is developed and improved through these three ingredients: *aggressiveness, positioning, and determination.* Combine these factors—even if you're not 6'11" and don't have good jumping ability—and you'll certainly be on your way to becoming an improved rebounder (Fig. 3-1).

How do you pick off all the loose balls that come from your teammates' (and your

3-2. Moses Malone moves toward the hoop for a possible offensive rebound and follow-up as he watches the flight of the ball.

own) missed shots? You have to try and anticipate where you think the ball will come off the rim and position yourself so that you will have a better chance to get the ball. The big problem is that you usually have a defensive man in front of you blocking and keeping you away from the basket. It always takes extra effort to establish good rebounding position, especially on offense.

One of the biggest mistakes young players make in rebounding is that, instead of going in for the rebound, they stand around, sometimes only for a moment, and watch the flight of the ball. If you or your teammate misses a shot, and you watch it first before going in for the rebound, you give the defense plenty of time to effectively box you out and keep you from getting anywhere near the basket (Fig. 3-2).

A good way to get out of the habit of watching shots before going in for the rebound is to automatically think that every shot that is taken will be missed. This will force you to anticipate where you think the shot will come off the rim.

Determination

WITH BUCK WILLIAMS
FORWARD;   6'8",   225 LB.

Buck Williams is only the eighth player in the history of the NBA to amass over a thousand rebounds in each of his first four seasons. Of all these rebounding greats, Williams is the only player to also score over 1,000 points in each of those four seasons. Williams was NBA Rookie of the Year in 1982.

My rebounding motto is "The ball belongs to me!" Rebounding on the offensive board is something that I've taken pride in throughout my basketball career. It takes a lot of hard work to be good at rebounding, but there's nothing more satisfying than a good rebound pulled down in a crowd under the glass, and then going back up with it, scoring *and* getting a foul shot too.

Mental outlook is one of the most important factors in rebounding. You need the proper frame of mind when going for the ball: you have to be determined that you will do your best to get the ball. Rebounding starts with determination. There are nine other players on the court, but you have to want to get the rebound the most. This mental and physical toughness will pay off.

Many times it's very common for the ball to come off the rim and not be grabbed right away. It may even bounce off your fingers, slip out of outstretched hands. A lot of times you have to go up two, maybe three times on one play just to get the rebound. Rebounding is always hard work, so don't give up now. By concentrating, going up that many times for the ball, and then finally coming down with it, and putting it back in the hole for two points, you can take the energy and heart right out of the other team.

3-3. Buck Williams goes up between two Chicago Bulls and pulls the rebound away.

One important thing to remember, especially for young players, is to rebound with two hands and then bring the ball down to your chest and spread out your elbows to protect the ball. When you try to grab the ball one-handed you won't have the total control you have when you rebound with two hands. Unless you're in a crowd situation and can only reach for the ball with one hand, stay away from one-handed rebounds (Fig. 3-3).

When you land on the floor with the ball, be sure to assume a wide and strong position. This will keep you from being knocked over when the defense bumps into you and also will better help you to protect the ball.

Positioning

WITH AKEEM OLAJUWON
CENTER;   7′0″,   250 LB.

After leading his University of Houston team to the NCAA final four in three collegiate seasons, Olajuwon was the first player selected in the 1984 college draft. In his rookie year he set the NBA season rebound high twice with 25. He finished the year with an 11.9-rpg average, the fourth best in the NBA, and was runner-up for Rookie of the Year honors.

Positioning for offensive rebounds is extremely important. When I was at the University of Houston, I used to jump for all the rebounds that I could, sometimes going over the backs of other players in order to get at the ball. But in the past few seasons I've worked very hard to improve my rebound positioning (Fig. 3-4).

A good strong position is the real secret of both offensive and defensive rebounding. First of all, you have to reach that spot in the lane where you think that the ball will come down, not too much under the basket, but not too far away from the rim either. I find that the best place is about four feet from the rim. Once you are here, you must be able to hold the position for two or three seconds. Keep low with bent knees, legs wide to provide a large and strong base. This will keep you from getting pushed away by the defense. Your back should be bent slightly forward and your arms held at a 45-degree angle over your shoulders. By holding your arms like this, the defense will not be able to hook you and pin your arms at your sides. You are now in good position to grab the rebound.

Remember, when you grab the rebound and come back down to the floor, don't try to dribble the ball. Immediately go back up strong to the basket with it or else pass it back out to a teammate.

3-4. Akeem Olajuwon has established good rebounding position against Louis Orr and waits for the ball to come off the hoop.

3-5. Ralph Sampson's determination and aggressiveness under the basket gets him many offensive rebounds.

Aggressiveness

WITH MOSES MALONE

The area under the backboard and out to the foul line ("the paint" as it's more commonly known around the NBA) is one of the most physical places in all the world of sport. When you're there, your job is to rebound. When I go in for a rebound in this area, I'm prepared to be elbowed, shoved, pushed, and even knocked to the ground. That's just the way the game is. If you're not willing to take the pain, you won't make any gains. Rebounding is a lot of hard work. I depend a lot on my upper-body strength to give me the power to push off and go to the hoop. If you don't fight for position, if you're too worried about contact under the boards, then you'll never become a great rebounder.

But even though it's so physical in the paint, whether on the pro, college, or high school level, a player still has to be extremely aggressive and go in there for the rebound. You have to do your best to get the position that you want and then hold your ground until the ball comes off the rim (Fig. 3-5). Whenever you are blocked out under the hoop by your defensive man, keep moving around and try for a better position.

Quickly note where your teammate has shot from, tell yourself that the ball won't go in, and move in with aggressiveness for rebounding position. Remember that 75 percent of all missed shots go in the direction away from the shooter. Generally, the further away the shooter is from the basket, the higher and further out the ball will bounce on the rebound. Shots taken from one side of the court have a tendency to bounce to the opposite side. Shots taken straight on at the basket will generally bounce straight back to the shooter. Study the way your teammates shoot and the type of arc that their shots have. This will tell you approximately where you can go for the rebound.

How to Go for the Offensive Rebound

WITH CLARK KELLOGG
FORWARD;   6'7",   230 LB.

After only four seasons, Clark Kellogg ranked ninth on the all-time Indiana Pacers rebound list. An All–Big Ten selection while at Ohio State University, Kellogg led the league in rebounding for two years. Kellogg was drafted in the first round by the Pacers in 1982. After leading Indiana in scoring, rebounding, and steals, he was runner-up for NBA Rookie of the Year honors.

WHEN NOT BLOCKED OUT

FAKE AND GO

If your defensive man is facing you as the ball goes up and hasn't begun to box you out, take a strong step in one direction, making a head-and-shoulder fake at the same time, followed by a change of direction and change of pace to go over him (Figs. 3-6a,b).

3-6a. Clark Kellogg fakes to his left as he prepares to go in for a rebound.

3-6b. Thanks to his faking, Kellogg is now in front of his defensive man and in good rebounding position.

WHEN BLOCKED OUT

REVERSE

If your defensive man has effectively blocked you out, you can lean with your shoulder on the middle of the defensive player's back. Using his back as a pivot, make a reverse by actually rolling around his back, placing your lead foot in front of his feet. If you do this correctly, you will end up standing in front of the defensive player.

OVER WITH THE ARMS

Arm movement is very important in helping you to establish rebounding position. When your defensive man has his arms raised up, raise your arms, hook one of them on the crook of his arm, and push it down. As you do this, step in front of him and take his position. If you can't get in front of him, at least try to get parallel with him so you will have a better chance to get the rebound (Figs. 3-7a,b).

Rebounding Drills

WITH CLARK KELLOGG

On a strictly physical level, rebounding is an explosive act that involves the contracting and tensing of the leg muscles and then jumping upward by straightening out those muscles. The higher you are able to jump, the better your chances of getting rebounds.

Not everyone has natural jumping ability, but everyone can improve what jumping capabilities they do possess.

The following drills will help improve your jumping ability and lateral movement, and therefore your rebounding.

LEG BOUNDS

This drill will develop strong muscles in your upper legs, giving you the explosive power needed to leap quickly and continuously for rebounds:

Stand at the end line on the basketball court with your legs together, arms at your sides, and knees bent so you're in a half squat. Jump out as far and as high as you can, thrusting with your arms and straightening out your body. When you land, land in the same crouched position and take off again with your next bound. Bound until you reach the end of the court. Rest for one to two minutes and then bound back. Do this two to five times per session.

3-7a. In this action Kareem Abdul-Jabbar uses his left arm to hold down the arm of Kelly Tripuka, effectively neutralizing him as a defensive threat.

3-7b. Jabbar has established a strong rebounding position and now can go up for the rebound with Tripuka behind him and out of the play.

SQUAT JUMPS

This drill will develop tremendous leg strength. Remember to jump as high as possible on each jump.

Stand on the basketball court with your feet shoulders'-width apart. Put your hands behind your head, lacing your fingers together. Drop to a half-squat position and then explode upward as high as possible, keeping your hands behind your head. When you land, begin the squat-and-jump process all over again. Do three sets of 25 repetitions with a rest of one to two minutes between sets.

STRING JUMPING

This drill will help develop quickness and power in your legs as well as increase endurance.

Place two chairs about four feet apart on the court and tie a piece of string between them about 12 to 18 inches high. Stand on one side of the string with your feet next to each other, legs flexed, arms held at your sides. Explode up and over the string using your legs and arms for power. Land on the balls of your feet. Once you land, repeat the motion and jump back over to the other side. Repeat the drill continuously for one minute, keeping track of how many jumps you performed. Do this drill three to five times with a one to two minute break between sets.

RIM TOUCHING

Stand under the basket and from a crouched position jump up and touch the rim. Once you come down, explode back up again. Set a target goal of 5 to 20 rim touches before taking a one to two minute rest period. Repeat the drill two to five times. If you can't touch the rim, face the backboard and pick out a spot on the backboard that you will try to touch.

BACKBOARD TOSSES

This drill will teach you to jump as high as you can for the ball and grab it with authority.

Stand about four feet from the front of the backboard, just off to the right or left of the rim. Throw the ball up underhanded at the middle of the side portion of the backboard. Once the ball makes contact with the backboard it will start to rise and come back toward you. Explode up toward the ball, trying for maximum height. When your fingers make contact with the ball, pull it into your chest and go down with it. Repeat this drill 10 to 20 times. Take a one to two minute rest between the three to five sets.

BACK TO THE BASKET

This drill will help develop power and quickness. You need a friend to help out on this drill.

Have your friend stand about six to eight feet from the backboard. You stand with your back to the backboard about four to six feet away. Have your friend throw the ball up underhanded. When you hear the ball hit the backboard, pivot, face the backboard, and spot the ball as quickly as possible. Jump up for it and pull in the rebound. Bring the ball down and then spring up with it for the follow-up shot. Repeat three sets of 10 to 15 times with a one to two minute rest between sets.

CONTINUOUS TAP-INS

You need two players to perform this drill. Start by facing the backboard, one player on the right side, the other to the left of the rim. The first player begins by tossing the ball over the rim to the opposite side of the backboard and then runs to that side. The second player jumps up and taps the ball over to the other side of the backboard and then quickly runs over to that side. Repeat this drill 20 times, rest for one minute, and repeat again.

LATERAL MOVEMENT DRILL

This is an excellent drill to enhance lateral movement, an important yet often neglected aspect of rebounding.

Begin this drill by standing four feet away from the backboard. Face the backboard with the basketball in your hands, one foot in the lane, the other foot just outside. Toss the ball up at the backboard over your head to the opposite side of the backboard. Quickly move and catch the ball with your arms extended before it hits the ground. Step back, once again keeping one foot in the lane and one foot out, and toss the ball back up again. Repeat 15 times, rest for one or two minutes, and repeat again.

4-1. Magic Johnson creates many offensive op-
portunities with his amazing passing ability.

CHAPTER 4

PASSING AND RECEIVING

Passing Sets Up the Winning Shots

WITH MAGIC JOHNSON
GUARD; 6'9", 222 LB.

After six seasons in the NBA, Earvin "Magic" Johnson had three Championship rings and was the NBA's all-time leader in assists in playoff competition. Magic was a true all-around player. In the 1981–82 season, he joined Wilt Chamberlain and Oscar Robertson as the third player to score more than 700 points, 700 rebounds, and 700 assists in the same season.

Passing the basketball is the quickest and most effective way to get the ball from player to player and move it around the court. The more passes that are made by the offense, the more you will challenge the defense and keep them scrambling, frustrated, and tired. The perfect end result of a series of well-executed passes will be a pass made to an open player close to the basket who just takes the ball and easily scores.

When you break the game of basketball down to its most elemental form, it's not the shooting that will win the game for you, it's the passing that went into setting up those winning shots.

I love to pass. It gives me a thrill to have the ball end up in the hands of the right player who's just ready to put it in the bucket for two points (Fig. 4-1).

Passing always involves two players: the one who throws the pass, and the one who is supposed to catch it. A pass, no matter how difficult or simple it is to make, is only good if it can be caught by your teammate. You can't overpower the ball or your teammate just won't be able to hold onto it. I try to make my passes soft enough so my man can catch the ball and then do something with it right away.

What I use for a target depends on the particular situation. With Kareem, because he's so tall, he'll hold up his hand and give me an easy target. With other players, I have to work harder, especially when I'm closely guarded. If my teammate is closely guarded, my target is his outside, open hand. When he's not closely guarded I aim the ball at the middle of his chest, right on his uniform numbers.

PASSES

The Two-Handed Chest Pass

WITH ISIAH THOMAS
GUARD;   6'1",   185 LB.

Thomas set the NBA all-time single-season record for assists when he finished the 1984–85 season with the Detroit Pistons with 1,123, well over 13 assists per game. In that same season he led the Pistons in assists for every game except one, failing to record double figures in only 12 contests. Thomas was selected by the fans to start in five consecutive NBA All-Star games, the only player in the league to do so. He was the Most Valuable Player in the 1984 game in Denver and the 1986 game in Dallas.

The chest pass is the most common pass you'll throw in a game when there isn't a defensive player between you and your teammate. To execute this pass, start with the ball held in two hands chest-high and close to your body. Your elbows should be tucked in and fingers spread around the ball with your thumbs up. Don't spread your fingers out too far because this positioning will prevent you from making a quick pass. As you hold the ball, your wrists should be pointed upward. Holding them downward will force you to first turn them up before you pass, an unnecessary extra movement that only delays the pass (Figs. 4-2a,b).

When you are about to make the pass, step out in the direction of the player you're passing to. Moving like this gives you body balance and therefore your pass has power and speed. But don't overextend the step or you will lose your balance. As your arms stretch out to their full length (you do this to obtain maximum power and to also shorten the distance between you and the receiver), rotate your elbows and wrists

4-2a. Isiah Thomas holds the ball properly as he prepares to throw a two-handed chest pass.

4-2b. As he releases the ball, arms and hands are extended with the palms turning outward.

outward so your hands end in a thumbs-downward, palms-out position. Release the ball with a snap of your wrists. Spin the ball with your index fingers, middle fingers, and thumbs as it goes out. This spin on the ball will cause it to travel in a straighter line, and make it much easier to catch than a "flat" (spinless) pass.

4-3a. Magic Johnson leans forward as he prepares to throw a bounce pass.

4-3b. At the end of the movement the fingers are spread, wrists and palms turning outward.

The Two-Handed Bounce Pass

WITH MAGIC JOHNSON

The basic mechanics of the bounce pass are the same as those of the chest pass, although the game situations when it is used are not. A bounce pass is a good one to make on a back-door play, when you are passing to a teammate guarded from behind in the low post by a much taller defender, or in other situations when you can't use the chest pass (Figs. 4-3a,b).

Starting with the same position as the two-handed chest pass, take a strong step in the direction of your teammate, quickly extending your arms and palms outward. Backspin, which makes the ball much easier to catch, will be put on the ball as you go from a thumbs up to a thumbs down position at the end of your release. The ball must hit the floor at least three-quarters of the distance to your teammate. It should come up to him at the level of his thighs and waist.

The Two-Handed Overhead Pass

WITH MAGIC JOHNSON

The overhead pass is commonly used for moving the ball around the perimeter, to pass the ball into the high and low post area, or as an outlet pass directly off a rebound to begin a fast break. When you make this pass, always aim the ball just a little over the head of the receiver (Figs. 4-4a,b).

To make an overhead pass hold the ball over your head, slightly back a little from the center of your head. Don't hold the ball behind your head; you waste movement and time. Your fingers should be firmly spread around the ball, thumbs a couple of inches apart from each other at the bottom of the ball. The pass gets its power from your wrist and fingers. As you step forward to release the ball—this will help you maintain your balance—snap your wrists and rotate both your arms and palms outward. Your hands should end with your fingers pointing upward.

The Lateral Pass

WITH MAGIC JOHNSON

The starting position is the same as for the two-handed chest pass. With your defender standing in front of you, step across the defender's body leading with the foot opposite the ball. This will protect the ball. Bring the ball to your side and extend your arms. Just before releasing the ball, bring the ball back, cock your wrist outside to add power to the pass, drop your helper hand, and then snap the ball to your teammate (Figs. 4-5a,b).

A variation of this pass is the lateral bounce pass, made with one or two hands. If you use this pass, the ball must be bounced to a spot at least three-quarters of the distance to the receiver (Fig. 4-6).

4-4a. Magic Johnson prepares to throw a two-hand overhead pass.

4-4b. This pass gets its power from the wrists and fingers. After you release the ball your hands should be pointing outward.

4-5a. Magic Johnson uses the lateral pass when his defender is standing in front of him, preventing him from passing straight ahead.

4-5b. The pass gets its power from your wrist. Cock your wrist back and then snap it just as you release the ball.

4-6. Isiah Thomas uses a lateral bounce pass to
get the ball into the low post.

The Push Pass

WITH MAGIC JOHNSON

The push pass is a quick pass made with one hand. The pass originates near your ear and relies on your elbow being bent for its power. It can be either a straight or a lob pass depending on the defensive alignment (Fig. 4-7).

4-7. Magic Johnson uses a push pass to get the ball to his teammate. Note how he has straightened out his arm and snapped his right wrist to give the ball its power.

The Baseball Pass

WITH BILL WALTON
CENTER;   6'11",   235 LB.

Bill Walton was rated as one of the most complete centers in the NBA. Unfortunately for him and basketball fans, he was injury-plagued throughout his NBA career. He led the Portland Trail Blazers to the NBA Championship in 1977 and in the following season he had his best year averaging just under 19 ppg and 13.2 rebounds. He was also selected as the NBA's Most Valuable Player that season despite missing 24 games with injuries. Playing for the Boston Celtics in 1985–86, he won the NBA's Sixth Man Award and helped the Celtics win the NBA Championship.

This is a long-distance pass that is usually thrown more than half the court length. Generally, one baseball pass to a player headed down-court ahead of the field is all that is needed to get a quick two points.

To make the baseball pass, keep both hands on the ball as long as possible so you can have better control. Also, this will enable you to stop the pass at the last moment if you have to. Plant your back foot and bring the ball back above the shoulder of your throwing arm. The arm must be bent at a 45-degree angle, with the upper arm nearly parallel to the floor. This position will enable you to throw a straight and quick pass. Step forward with the foot opposite your throwing arm and follow through overhead with the ball. As you release the ball with one hand you should snap your wrist, and your arm should be fully extended. Remember not to put the ball completely behind your head. This will save you both time and movement (Figs. 4-8*a,b,c*).

Put a back rotation on the pass to make the trajectory of the ball straight and easier to catch. End the movement with the arm completely stretched out, the palm facing outward perpendicular to the floor, and the thumb pointed toward the floor.

The Behind-the-Back Pass

WITH REGGIE THEUS
GUARD;   6'7",   208 LB.

Reggie Theus was named to the NBA All-Rookie team in 1980 after a successful career at the University of Nevada, Las Vegas. He was selected for the All-Star game in 1981 and 1983.

This pass was once considered to be a fancy pass but has now come to be a normal offensive weapon in the NBA. It must not be abused.

4-8a. Bill Walton winds up and prepares to throw a baseball pass. The ball is well protected from defenders by his flared elbows.

4-8b. He steps forward with the leg opposite
from his throwing arm and releases the ball.

4-8*c.* **Full extension of the arm and hand ensures
a better pass.**

To make this pass, hold the ball with two hands. As you bring the ball back around your hip, your helping hand drops off. Your passing hand is on the side of the ball and it must thrust the ball behind the back. The movement ends with the passing hand near the opposite hip, with the fingers pointing in the direction of the pass.

The Hand-Off Pass

WITH MAGIC JOHNSON

This is a pass that doesn't require an extension of the arm and is used for giving the ball to a player who is either cutting or circling behind you. The ball is held with one hand up and the other under the ball so it's easier for the teammate to catch the ball while cutting. This pass can also be made by holding the ball and simply flipping it to a nearby teammate (Fig. 4-9). Another variation is to turn your body toward the receiver or else make a complete turn and face the receiver and then give him the ball.

The Hook Pass

WITH MAGIC JOHNSON

When you are closely guarded, hold the ball at shoulder level, elbows flared outward to protect the ball. Start to lift the ball up with two hands with the wrist of the outside passing hand flexed. Drop your helping hand to face level and extend your passing arm over your head with the ball. When you have stretched this arm out completely, flick the ball by snapping your wrist forward.

The Off-the-Dribble Pass

WITH MAGIC JOHNSON

This is becoming a pass that is popping up more and more at every level of basketball. To make this pass work, on your last dribble of the ball, move your dribbling hand to the top quarter of the ball, combine a lateral movement of the hand and arm, and push the ball forward with a snap of the wrist toward your teammate. The pass is a quick and deceptive one that will usually catch your defensive man by surprise (Fig. 4-10).

4-9. Magic Johnson uses a gentle flip pass to get the ball to his favorite receiver, Kareem Abdul-Jabbar.

4-10. Magic Johnson effectively uses an off-the-dribble pass while running at full speed. The pass gets its power when you extend your arm and then snap your wrist as you release the ball.

The Five Passing Lanes

WITH MAGIC JOHNSON

Each game situation presents the possibility for one perfect pass. Imagine yourself faced by a defender crouched over in good defensive position. What you should now see is not just this player but actually five possible passing lanes. These five lanes are:

1. over the top of the defender's head

2. near the left side of his head

3. near the right side of his head

4. near his right leg

5. near his left leg

If you are well guarded by your man you won't be able to pass the ball immediately where you want to. In cases like this, fake with the ball, fake with your body, or fake with your body and the ball. Once the defender goes for the fake, pass through one of the five lanes (Fig. 4-11).

Catching the Ball

WITH NORM NIXON

GUARD;   6'2",   175 LB.

Norm Nixon, a prolific scorer, registered 32 ''double doubles'' (double figures in assists and points) in the 1984–85 season with the L. A. Clippers. That season he also ranked eighth on the NBA's all-time assist list with a total of 5,471. In 1980 and 1982 Nixon helped guide the Los Angeles Lakers to the NBA Championship title.

A pass is only good if it can be caught. Therefore you should be always ready to catch the ball, anticipating both when and where the pass will be thrown. In order to catch the ball you should:

• Get as open as possible and present a good target to the passer. To receive the ball, keep your hands out from your chest, fingers pointed up. Between the passer and the receiver there is an unspoken signal to pass the ball: the raised and open hands of the receiver. Your fingers should be spread comfortably, thumbs almost

4-11. Clyde Drexler has Magic Johnson covered, blocking off some of his passing lanes. A fake is all that's needed to open up the passing lane that you want.

4-12. Bill Walton presents a very good target as
he prepares to receive the ball in front of Darryl
Dawkins.

touching each other. This position enables you to immediately get a good solid grip on the ball when you receive it (Fig. 4-12).

- Not every pass will be textbook perfect. Be ready to move from side to side for a poorly thrown or deflected pass.

- Keep your eyes on the ball from the time it leaves your teammate's hands until you actually touch the ball yourself. Taking your eyes off the ball for only a half second can result in a dropped or fumbled pass.

- Step toward the ball as it comes to you with your arms out to decrease the length of the pass and to prevent the defense from stepping in and stealing the ball.

- After the ball hits your fingers, bend your elbows slightly and bring the ball in toward your chest. This cushions the impact of the pass and gives you better control of the ball.

- By already having the ball at chest level, you are now in position to pass or shoot quickly.

Passing Drills

Passing, like shooting, is developed through constant practice. By regularly working on the following drills your passing mechanics will surely improve. However, it's only through team practice sessions, with your coach watching, as well as during games, that you will really learn *when* to pass and *how* to get the pass over, under, or through outstretched defensive hands. These situations are the ones that will develop and sharpen your passing skills the most, turning your passing mechanics into valuable on-court skills.

WALL PASSING

One of the first drills to work on is the wall drill. This will help you develop your two-handed chest pass as well as the bounce pass. Performing the drill regularly will improve your reflexes and form, and help you develop ball rotation and arm strength.

Stand approximately six feet from a wall and pass the ball chest-high to a spot you have marked out on the wall. Concentrate on your form. After twenty passes, step back two feet and take twenty more chest passes. Repeat the drill using bounce passes.

Toward the end of this drill your arms may begin to get tired and your fingertips might even become sore from passing the ball so much. But keep concentrating and maintaining your form throughout the drill.

As a final part to the drill, see how many chest passes or bounce passes you can make in 60 seconds. Try to increase the number at each practice session.

DEAD BALL

When you play with your teammates or friends, play with the rule that dribbling is not allowed. If you do dribble, you lose possession of the ball. By playing with this "dead ball" rule all players will be forced to concentrate on their passing game and look for the open man instead of dribbling the ball.

BULL IN THE RING

Form a circle with players standing at least four feet from each other. Place one defensive man in the middle. The object of this drill is to pass the ball to each other without the defensive man touching, deflecting, or stealing the ball. In this case, the passer who makes the mistake becomes the defender and the defender goes on offense. The one rule to this game is that you are not allowed to pass to players standing on either side of you.

TWO ON ONE

Two offensive players with one ball line up across from each other at the half court or free-throw circle. One defensive man stands in the middle of the circle, trying to touch, deflect, or steal the ball. Using fakes, the two passers must pass the ball to each other without dribbling or taking steps. Once the ball is touched by the defender, the passer goes in the middle and the defender becomes a passer.

5-1. Rickey Green keeps the ball low to the floor, protecting it from his defensive man with his hip and his right arm.

CHAPTER 5

DRIBBLING

It Has to Have Purpose

WITH ISIAH THOMAS

In basketball there are two ways to move the ball. The preferred manner is with a pass because it's much quicker. But if the defense is tight and all passing lanes are clogged, you can move the ball by using a dribble to set up the offense.

Since you can only begin and stop the dribble one time for each possession, you have to make your dribbling count; *it has to have purpose.*

Dribbling, along with passing and shooting, is one of the triple offensive threats you have in your basketball arsenal. Use the dribble to move the ball on offense; to blow past your man to the hoop; to escape from a tough, sticky defense; to shoot, or to move around a screen and get off your shot from behind it; to get a better passing angle; to freeze the ball in the closing minutes of a half.

Don't pound the air out of the basketball while going nowhere. If you want to get from point A to point B on the court, do it with the least amount of dribbling possible. Once you put the ball down on the floor it has to help you get where you want to go. If the dribble can't help you, look for someone to pass to.

The mistake that I see many young players make on the court is that they just dribble too much. Many of these players don't realize they're hogging the ball because they're too intent on their own dribbling. But while they're playing with the ball, four other teammates are standing around waiting for something to happen. Before you know it, the defense begins to tighten up. More often than not the dribbler then gets trapped and turns the ball over to the defense, which often runs the ball back down-court for an easy two points.

How to Dribble

WITH ISIAH THOMAS

Contrary to what many young players actually do, dribbling is *not* done while staring at the ball with your eyes. You dribble only with your fingertips and the pads of your hands, without looking at the ball. Keep your head up at all times and your eyes focused on the court and what's going on. A properly inflated round basketball bounced off the floor will always bounce straight up at least 75 percent of the height from which it was dropped. Therefore, you don't have to watch the ball as you dribble. "See" with your fingertips. Just have your fingers there to meet and control the ball.

To dribble, push the ball down by spreading the fingers and flexing the wrist. You don't need to push it down hard; light pressure is enough. Also, keep your legs flexed and your back straight so you're ready to make a quick move.

All players should learn to dribble equally well with both hands. This ambidextrous ability will greatly open up your offensive game by preventing the defense from trying to overplay you on your strong side; both your sides are strong when you can dribble with either hand.

TYPES OF DRIBBLES

The Low Dribble

WITH RICKEY GREEN

The low dribble is used whenever you are closely guarded. This type of dribbling simply entails keeping the ball low to the floor and in your control. Extend your dribbling hand and arm down as much as possible to shorten the distance the ball has to travel. Keep the elbow of your dribbling hand close in at your side. Dribble the ball on the side of your body away from the defender. The palm of your dribbling hand is kept over the ball. Don't watch the ball as you dribble; look over the court and prepare your options (Fig. 5-1).

Use your other forearm to shield the ball from the defender. While being tightly guarded, be careful not to blatantly push or shove the defender with your forearm or you'll be whistled for an offensive foul.

The Speed Dribble

WITH RICKEY GREEN

Once you're in the open court you need to go as fast as you can with the ball while still remaining in control of the ball and your body. Since you're not tightly guarded by the defense, keeping the ball from the defenders isn't a priority here—maintaining top speed is. To run fast and dribble at the same time, push the ball out in front of you at waist height and run after it, keeping your head up so you can see the entire court, your teammates, and whatever defenders are in front of you. The faster you run, the farther out in front of you the ball has to be pushed. With this type of dribble, your hand is not directly over the ball as in the low dribble, but behind it (at nearly a 45-degree angle to the floor) so you can push the ball hard and in front of you with your arm completely extended.

The speed dribble requires a high dribble, but make sure that the bounce is not higher than hip level or else you may lose control of the ball as you sprint down-court.

The Change-of-Pace Dribble

WITH RICKEY GREEN

This dribble is one of the most common ones in basketball and is used to make the defender think that you're slowing down or going to pick up your dribble and stop.

When your man is closely guarding you, slow your dribble down and almost come to a stop. Straighten up your back as if you are looking for a teammate to pass to, but still keep your dribble. Once the man guarding you loosens up his defense, quickly bend over, dribble the ball out hard and long, and explode by him at top speed, protecting the ball with your free hand as you move around him. The dribbling hand slides from the top of the ball to behind it, to nearly a 45-degree angle to the floor. This allows you to push the ball hard.

5-2a. Isiah Thomas is looking to his right, but is actually preparing to move quickly to his left with a crossover dribble.

The Crossover Dribble

WITH ISIAH THOMAS

The crossover dribble entails dribbling with one hand, then, as you get close to your defender, pushing the ball out in front of you, over to the other hand, and exploding

5-2b. Staying low and keeping the ball close to the floor, Thomas changes direction and runs Brad Davis off a well-made screen.

past him. This move is a very good way to lose your defender, but, since the ball is unprotected as you make the crossover, it can be stolen by the defense if the move isn't done smoothly.

Keep the ball low as you dribble. If you are dribbling with your right hand, once you get close to the defender, bounce it over to your left side near your left foot. The right hand must be kept on the side of the ball in order to push it over. Keep your left hand ready to receive the ball with your palm held perpendicular to the floor for a split second to stop the movement of the ball and then push the ball out in front of you (Fig. 5-2a,b). Stay low, shifting your weight by pushing toward your new direction with the inside of your right foot. Lower your right shoulder and use your trunk to protect the ball from the defense. Cut as close to your defender as possible. For best results, combine the crossover dribble with a change of pace.

The Between-the-Legs Dribble

WITH ISIAH THOMAS

This dribble is a quick way to move the ball from one hand to another when you are closely guarded or when being overplayed and you want to change dribbling direction (Fig. 5-3).

Let's assume you are dribbling with your right hand and want to change over to your left. Keep your dribble low. On the last dribble you take before the changeover, put your right hand laterally on the outside of the ball and push it hard between your spread legs. Your left hand must be close to your legs to receive the ball with the fingers spread out and pointed to the floor. Continue dribbling with your left hand.

The Reverse Dribble

WITH NORM NIXON

This dribble is used when you are closely guarded. Its major drawback is that the dribbler will momentarily lose sight of his own teammates and other defenders while the move is being made.

As you dribble toward the defender, stop hard for about a half second. Using your left foot as the pivot (assuming you are dribbling right-handed), stay low and turn your back on your defender. To do this without walking, move your right leg, right shoulder, and head to the left while pivoting on your left foot. Keep dribbling with your right hand as you pivot on your left foot. To maintain proper balance, don't keep your feet close to each other as you pivot. The right foot must be turned and pointed quickly in the new

5-3. Isiah Thomas uses the between-the-legs dribble to change his dribbling direction. His legs are comfortably spread and his left hand is set to receive the ball as it comes between his legs.

direction to assist the rest of your body in making the turn. For quick execution of the move, swing your right arm and shoulder to help with your rotation. Shift the right hand from the top of the ball over to your right side, pushing the ball from the side and swinging it around. Slap the ball hard on the floor with your first bounce. It must pass laterally over your left foot. The dribble is then continued with the left hand.

The Half-Reverse Dribble

WITH NORM NIXON

Start this move just as you would the normal reverse dribble, make a 90-degree turn and then come back to your original position. To be effective, the move must be done quickly. Keep your palm on the side of the ball for the first 90-degree turn and then switch it to the other side of the ball when you bring it back to the starting position.

The Hockey Dribble

WITH ISIAH THOMAS

The hockey dribble is a staggered dribble move, used to throw off a defender, that combines a head-and-shoulder fake and a change of pace. To make this move, stay low and keep the ball at your side. As you get close to the defender, make small "stutter" steps (short, quick, parallel steps) with your feet. At the same time make head-and-shoulder fakes to confuse the defense. If you're dribbling with your right hand, fake to the left with your left foot and left shoulder, continuing your dribble at the same time. Then quickly cut back, pick up speed, and push the ball out with your right hand. Move past the defender with your right leg leading the way. In some situations you may want to then use a crossover dribble to get by your man.

The Behind-the-Back Dribble

WITH ISIAH THOMAS

As you approach the defender on the right side, change your direction slightly to the left to make the move past the defender on your left. After you have taken your last dribble with your right hand, slide your palm over and then outside on the ball, swinging it behind and across your lower back, pushing the ball to your left side. End the movement of your right arm as close to your left hip as possible. This will give you the most ball control. Once you have control of the ball with your left hand, increase your tempo as you make the first dribble.

To make this move work really well, it's important that the first bounce on the left side be made way out in front and to the side of the left foot.

The Backup Dribble

WITH ISIAH THOMAS

This is mainly a dribbling move used to escape a dangerous defensive situation. When dribbling with your right hand, turn your shoulder to the defender, push back on your left foot away from the defender, and simultaneously make a dribble back. Protect the ball with your left shoulder and arm (Fig. 5-4).

5-4. Dennis Johnson uses a backup dribble to escape the defensive trap of Byron Scott.

Ball Handling and Dribbling Drills

WITH ISIAH THOMAS

Dribbling is a skill that is only developed after many hours of having the ball in your hands. As with all offensive basketball moves, your dribbling skills will only improve through hard work. When you practice dribbling, avoid as much as possible the temptation to look at the ball. An excellent drill for beginners is to simply take a basketball with you everywhere you go. Dribble the ball as you walk to school or go over to visit a friend. The next time you go out for a jog, take the ball with you and dribble it the entire distance. After some time you'll be dribbling the ball without looking at it because you've made it such a natural and instinctive act that you don't even think about it.

Once you are adept with dribbling the ball without looking at it, start to work on the specific dribbling maneuvers (behind-the-back dribble, between-the-legs dribble, etc.) to perfect your court skills. It's important to remember that you first have to learn the actual dribbling mechanics of each move before trying to make the dribble move at game speed. All the top NBA guards can each make dribble moves look simple during a game as they move seemingly without effort on the court. But each one of these players started out when they were younger by *slowly* practicing the dribble moves, increasing the speed little by little only after becoming comfortable with the ball and the move at slow speed.

Here are some simple ball-handling and dribbling drills that you can work on by yourself to help increase your dribbling proficiency and ball-handling ability.

AROUND THE LEGS

Keep your feet shoulders'-width apart. Flex your knees and bend over at your waist. Holding the ball in your right hand, move it between your legs and around your left knee. Pick the ball up with your left hand, swing it around to the front of your left knee and back to your right hand. Repeat. Do 15 to 25 repetitions of this drill on your left leg and then repeat it on your right leg.

AROUND THE KNEES

Keep your feet a few inches apart from each other, flex your knees, and bend at the waist. Holding the ball in your right hand, pass it behind your knees to your left hand. Pass the ball around the front of your knees with your left hand to your right hand. Repeat this drill 15 to 25 times going in one direction as quickly as possible. Change direction and repeat the drill again.

AROUND THE WAIST

Stand up straight with your feet shoulders'-width apart. Hold the ball at waist level in your right hand and pass it behind your back as far as possible to your left hand. Pass the ball around the front of your waist as far as possible to your right hand. Repeat the drill 15 to 25 times going as quickly as possible. Change direction and repeat the drill again.

THE FIGURE-8

Keep your feet spread wider than shoulders' width, flex your knees, and bend forward at the waist. Holding the ball at knee level in your right hand, pass it behind your left leg to your left hand. Pass it around the front of your left leg to behind your right knee to your right hand. Pass it around the front of your right knee to the back of your left knee. Repeat the drill 10 to 15 times going as quickly as possible. Change direction and repeat the drill. Don't watch the ball as you do the drill.

FIGURE-8 WITH DROP IN THE MIDDLE

This drill is done exactly as the figure eight except each time that you bring the ball between your legs from the front, drop it. Picking it up off the bounce, continue the drill as before. Repeat the drill 10 to 15 times going as quickly as possible. Change direction and repeat the drill again.

BETWEEN-THE-LEGS RUN

This ball-handling drill is a good prelude to the between-the-legs dribbling drill. Assume a crouched position and begin moving slowly down-court. As you move, pass the ball quickly from your right hand between your legs to the back of your left leg to your left hand. With your left hand, pass the ball around the front of your left leg, between your legs to the back of your right leg to your right hand. Repeat the drill continuously while moving down-court. Don't watch the ball.

BETWEEN-THE-LEGS BOUNCE
AND CATCH

Holding the ball over your head with two hands, spread your feet slightly further than shoulders' width. Swing the ball forward and bounce it on the floor between your legs near your heels. Swing your arms back quickly and catch the ball with your two hands as it bounces up toward your hips. Repeat the drill 10 to 15 times as quickly as possible.

BALL DROP/HAND CLAP

Here's a tricky drill that requires quickness and, since you won't be looking at the ball, a sense of where the ball is. Flex your knees, keep your feet together, and bend forward at the waist. Holding the ball behind your knees, let it drop to the floor. Bring your hands to the front of your knees, clap them together, then quickly bring them behind your knees to pick the ball up before the next bounce. Repeat this drill 10 to 15 times.

SIT DRIBBLING

Sit on the floor with your legs crossed in front of you. With the ball in your right hand, begin to dribble it around your back as far over to your left hip as possible. Pass it to your left hand and continue dribbling in front of you as far as you can to your right hip. Repeat the drill 10 to 15 times and then switch directions.

FULL-COURT SPEED DRIBBLE

Move quickly down the court with the ball waist-high and far out in front of you. Make the lay-up and head back up-court, repeating the speed dribble and lay-up. Do this 4 to 6 times and take a short rest. Repeat.

CROSSOVER DRIBBLE

Set up a series of folding chairs or cones on the basketball court about 10 to 15 feet apart. Pretend that they are defensive players trying to grab at the ball. Begin at one end of the basketball court and dribble around the chairs, weaving your way to the end. As you approach each chair, change your dribbling hand, remembering to keep the ball low and close to your body.

REVERSE DRIBBLE

Place three chairs 15 feet apart on the court and pretend that they are defensive players. Dribble toward them and make your spin move, using proper form and technique. When you arrive at the next chair, repeat the move. On your return trip down the court, try making the move with your opposite hand.

CHAPTER 6

SHOOTING

The Joys of Shooting

WITH KIKI VANDEWEGHE
FORWARD; 6'8", 220 LB.

In six NBA seasons Vandeweghe registered .540 in field-goal shooting accuracy to go along with his 23.1 scoring average. He led the Portland Trail Blazers in scoring in 1985–86, finishing with a 24.8-ppg average for the year.

Shooting is the most practiced fundamental skill in basketball, and with good reason. A team can run a play to perfection, but they still need players to execute the final part: putting the ball in the basket. And because even the best NBA shooters will only score on half of the shots they take in a game, shooting will always have to be practiced daily.

Although practically everyone in the NBA can shoot well, not everyone is a scorer. Being a scorer is what separates the All-Stars from the good shooters. A scorer is someone who will make the shot when he's open and within his range and will work the hardest to get in position to get his shot. A scorer is also able to make things happen for himself offensively on the court by using fakes and screens to his advantage. But most importantly, when the game is on the line, a scorer is the player that everyone will look to. He can be counted on to score the basket for them when it's needed the most.

Always knowing which shots you can take—a jumper, hook shot, or a driving lay-up—and when you can take them in the course of a game is what I consider to be the mark of a good scorer.

In basketball, shooting the ball is the first thing that any kid wants to do. I've never heard of someone going to the court to "rebound a few baskets"; it's always to "shoot a few baskets." Like getting a good solid hit in baseball or scoring a winning touchdown in football, shooting and sinking baskets has its own special magic that can grip you and never let you go. The more you score when you're on the court, the better you feel about the game and about yourself.

Shooting never will become easy, even for a professional player. Each and every shot you'll take in a game has its own particular challenge. Each basket scored becomes a reward for the work that you put into the shot. But then, there is the next basket to be scored, and the next one after that.

I think that shooting is best practiced alone—just you and a basketball. If you are willing to stick with it, those long, solitary hours with the ball will eventually pay off. After combining sound shooting fundamentals with those hundreds of hours of shooting practice, one day you'll end up in a full-court game standing on your favorite spot on the court with the ball in your hands. Just like you've done so many times in practice, you'll fake your man, dribble by him, and go up for your shot. With your shooting arm extended out, you'll watch as the ball swishes through the net. There's no better feeling in the game than this, and it makes all the work involved seem so worthwhile.

THE DIFFERENT SHOTS

The Lay-Up

WITH REGGIE THEUS

In the game of basketball, a lay-up is the first shot that should be learned. In a competitive situation, this is the one shot that you have to be able to make with your right hand when you're on the right side of the court and your left hand when you're on the left side of the court. It's the lay-up, more than any other shot in basketball, that puts you closest to the basket. Unless you are fouled (and even then you should still try to make the shot) when going in for a lay-up, there is no reason for you ever to miss this shot (Fig. 6-1a,b,c).

Here's how to make a lay-up on the right side of the basket. Dribble towards the basket. When you're several feet away from the hoop, simultaneously put your left foot on the ground, take your last dribble, and bring your right knee up very quickly. The higher the knee lift on this powerful thrusting move, the closer you will be lifted up towards the basket.

6-1a. Reggie Theus holds the ball close to his chest as he prepares to go in for a lay-up.

6-1*b***. He plants his foot . . .**

6-1c. . . . and goes straight up to the hoop.

Almost at the same time that your left foot is planted on the ground and you have started to lift your right leg, use both hands and swing the ball up from your hips straight out in front of your head. Drop your non-shooting hand when the ball is at the level of your forehead. You can now use this helping arm for defensive purposes. The ball should now be resting on the palm of your right hand, which is nearly parallel to the floor.

When you are close to the backboard and at the peak of your jump, flick the wrist and lay the ball softly near the upper corner of the painted box. Carried by the momentum generated from your arm movement, the ball should gently roll off your fingertips, hit the backboard and fall into the basket.

A common beginner's mistake is to jump out instead of up when going in for a lay-up, which prevents you from getting high off the ground on your shot. This problem is easily corrected by lifting your right knee as high as possible as you jump towards the hoop.

The Reverse Lay-Up

WITH LARRY DREW
GUARD;   6'2",   190 LB.

Drew registered nine double doubles (double figures in assists and scoring) and scored in double figures in 64 of the 72 games he played in the 1984–85 season. The first-round pick from the University of Missouri in 1980, Drew also had an NBA career scoring high of 33 points against Houston in 1983.

This lay-up has the benefit of the rim and backboard to help protect you from defenders trying to block your shot from behind. It's a good shot to use after a penetration on the baseline or when you receive the ball inside the lane with your back to the basket.

The last two steps of the reverse lay-up are the same as those described before for the regular lay-up. As you take your last step for the reverse, however, bring the ball up, over, and then behind your head with two hands. Slide your shooting hand around the ball, give a backspin to it and toss the ball up to the upper right corner of the painted box on the backboard (Fig. 6-2).

A common mistake that I've seen young players make is to try to make this shot while holding the ball with only one hand. Unfortunately their hands aren't large or strong enough and the ball often slips out of their grasp.

6-2. Larry Drew uses the reverse lay-up many times to keep his defender from blocking his shot from behind.

THE JUMP SHOT

Body Balance

WITH KIKI VANDEWEGHE

Of all the shots taken in a basketball game, the jump shot is the most widely used in a player's offensive arsenal. Since it is taken at the highest point of the shooter's vertical jump, it's a shot that's extremely hard to block. The jump part of the shot also provides the shooter with much more shooting range because the leg muscles help power the ball out further. In the pros and in college, many players are effective with their jump shot from as far away as 25 feet.

The proper jump shot is all based on body balance. When you're properly balanced, your body motion won't have any bad effect on the mechanics of your shot. For proper balance, hold the ball comfortably in your hands, then square your shoulders in the direction of the basket. Your feet should be shoulders'-width apart, with the foot on the side of your shooting hand out a little in front of the other. This will give you a wider base and therefore better balance. If you were to draw a line from the center of your two feet to the basket there would be a straight line. The reason for jumping with both your feet and body aimed at the basket is that you will now be able to get full power from your leg muscles. Your body will also be properly balanced, and therefore all body muscles will be able to give a coordinated effort (Fig. 6-3).

Bend your knees and balance your body weight evenly and comfortably on both your feet. The bent knee stance keeps you limber, ready to move. It will also provide you with the initial powerful muscular thrust to drive you by your man or up into the air for your jump shot (Figs. 6-4a,b).

Arm and Hand Position

WITH MIKE MITCHELL
FORWARD;   6'7",   215 LB.

A first-round draft choice by Cleveland in 1978 from Auburn, Mitchell scored 14 points in 15 minutes in the 1982 All-Star game in addition to dishing out two assists and grabbing four rebounds. As of 1986, Mitchell was a lifetime 20-ppg scorer, and his high game in the NBA was 47 points.

The shooting arm must be flexed, held near the body, with the forearm nearly parallel to the floor. The helper arm must be at a near 45-degree angle, with the elbow pointing slightly outward.

6-3. Kiki Vandeweghe prepares for a jump shot. By being properly balanced as he goes up, he ensures that his body movement won't have any bad effect on the mechanics of his shot.

6-4*a*. Larry Bird bends his knees slightly as he prepares to take a jump shot.

6-4*b*. His follow-through is perfect: shooting hand extended, wrist cocked, and fingers pointing to the hoop.

The shooting hand must be cocked back toward your chest as much as possible with the fingers spread out comfortably, the ball resting on the pads of your fingers. This positioning offers the best ball control and allows the fingers—not the palm—to push the ball toward the hoop (Figs. 6-5*a,b*).

Don't keep the ball on the middle or back of the palm. The hand must be held under the ball and slightly to the outside. Keep your index finger, or guide finger, in the middle of the basketball (Fig. 6-6).

The helper hand is held to the side of the ball, nearly perpendicular to the floor. Don't put your helper hand in front of the ball because this will change the trajectory of your shot. The helper hand does just what its name implies: it only helps or assists in lifting the ball before you take a shot. Shooting must be a smooth, fluid motion combining your legs, midsection, upper body, and arm extension. Your shoulder, elbow, and hand should be on the same vertical line with each other (Fig. 6-7). If you make the mistake of not pointing the elbow of your shooting arm toward the basket, it will adversely affect the trajectory of your shot. When you jump, be sure to extend your legs out as you are extending your arm. If not, you won't be able to release the ball at the peak of your jump and therefore you won't be able to get full power out of your shot.

In the Air

WITH WALTER DAVIS
GUARD;   6'6",   200 LB.

Rookie of the Year in 1977–78, Davis holds an NBA record for scoring 34 points in a row without a miss, hitting 15 straight field goals and four free throws in a February 25, 1983, game against Seattle. This five-time NBA All-Star has a career scoring high of 43 points.

While you are going up for your shot, release the helper hand from the ball just a little over your forehead and bring the ball up and out with only the shooting hand (Fig. 6-8).

When you are at the peak of your jump (it's not important how high you jump, but rather how balanced you are), you must snap the wrist of your shooting hand toward the basket with the palm nearly parallel to the floor and the index finger pointed toward the middle of the rim.

The three most important fingers on your shooting hand are the thumb, index, and middle, while the two other fingers are used only for balance. For this reason, the final direction of these three fingers at the end of your shot will determine the ultimate direction of your shot (Fig. 6-9).

6-5a. Mike Mitchell cocks the ball back with his wrist. The elbow of his helper arm is pointing slightly outward.

6-5*b*. The ball is resting on the pads of his fingers and the fingers are spread comfortably to provide the best control.

6-6. Accurate shooting depends on finger-tip control. With the ball resting on the pads of your fingers, there should be space between the ball and your palm. This sim-ple test will show you if you are shooting properly, with your fingers and not with your palm.

6-7. Mike Mitchell demonstrates a smooth, fluid shooting motion on his jump shot.

**6-8. Walter Davis exhibits perfect body balance
as he goes up for his jump shot.**

6-9. Larry Bird has his eyes focused on the rim as he releases his jump shot against Bobby Jones.

The Follow-Through

WITH DARRELL GRIFFITH
GUARD;   6'4",   190 LB.

Griffith, star of the 1980 NCAA–championship University of Louisville team, won the NBA Rookie of the Year award the following year. He has scored 20-plus points per game in four of his five pro seasons. An all-around player, Griffith ranks in the top three for the Utah Jazz in most offensive categories, including points, field goals, and field-goal attempts.

In all sports, from baseball to tennis to football to hockey, the follow-through motion in the shooting or passing movement is extremely important. The same is true in basketball. Once the ball is released, follow through with your shot by fully extending your shooting arm. There are two reasons for this. First of all, this movement will shorten the distance that the basketball has to travel to the basket. Secondly, you are aiming at the target, which can be either the backboard or the rim. Your follow-through motion reinforces this aim.

The Arc of the Shot

WITH WORLD B. FREE
GUARD;   6'3",   190 LB.

Free has an 11-year 21.4-ppg scoring average with a high game of 49 points. Playing for the Cleveland Cavaliers in the 1984–85 season in one of their rare playoff appearances, Free averaged 26 ppg with a high of 32 points against the Celtics in game three, equaling a Cav single-game team playoff record.

When I was a young kid back in Brooklyn I started putting a high arc on my shot to keep it from getting knocked back by the taller players at the playground. Little did I realize then that this is the best way to shoot. All good shooters will always arc their shots. Arcing the ball and putting a backspin on the shot will help "soften" the shot when it hits the rim or the backboard, causing it to lose speed and force, giving the ball a higher possibility of falling into the hoop (Fig. 6-10).

But above all, if you arc the ball, the chances of it going in are much higher than if you took a line-drive shot. The basket is actually large enough for two basketballs to fit

6-10. World B. Free launches one of his high-
arcing jumpers.

into it at the same time. If you put a good arc on your shot, the ball will go up, over, and then come down toward the rim. Even if you're slightly off with your shot you will have a greater chance of having the ball go in because your target area is still a large one.

The Target

WITH PURVIS SHORT
FORWARD;   6'7",   215 LB.

Short has an 18.7-ppg career scoring average for eight seasons of play with a high of 59 points coming in the 1984–85 season against New Jersey. In the 1985–86 season, he averaged 25.5-ppg.

THE RIM

A shooter can have two targets: the rim and the backboard. When you go up for your jump shot, fix your eyes on the back part of the rim (the part nearest to the backboard). This is also the preferred target for many other players. If your shot hits there, the backspin put on the ball at the final stage of your shot will slow the ball down, lessen its impact when it hits, and cause it to linger momentarily and then fall backward into the hoop. Also, if your shot should happen to fall a little short of the back rim, it will go right into the basket instead. And if the ball should go too far, it may still go in after bouncing off the backboard.

When you aim for the front of the rim, you don't have any of these options.

THE BACKBOARD

Whenever you are on the court at an angle to the rim, you should try to make use of the backboard for your jump shot, because it will make your chances of making the shot much greater than if you just shot directly at the rim. I concentrate on hitting the upper corner of the painted box on the side I am shooting from. The bank shot is a soft shot, so don't overpower the ball.

6-11. Rolando Blackman going to shoot a jump shot off the dribble. This is a quick move that often catches a defender unprepared to defend against it.

Back on the Floor

WITH WALTER DAVIS

Land on both feet, slightly out ahead from where you jumped. If you land too far back or off to the side, this means you are leaning in one of those directions with some part of your body when you go up for the shot. All it takes is a slight lean to throw your shot off.

As soon as you land on the floor, move into position to go for the rebound.

The Jump Shot after the Dribble

WITH ROLANDO BLACKMAN
GUARD;   6'6",   194 LB.

Called "the best guard I ever coached" by Dallas Maverick coach, Dick Motta, Blackman averaged 32.8 ppg for the 1984–85 playoffs, an NBA high that season. Blackman has a five-year NBA career high of 43 points, a .516 field-goal shooting accuracy, and has never fouled out of an NBA game. He was selected to the NBA All-Star team in 1985 and 1986.

The jump shot taken after a dribble has a different beginning when you compare it to a stationary jump shot or a jump shot taken right after a pass. If you are right-handed, make a two-count stop. Your left foot is the first foot to hit the floor. Land on your heel and begin to roll forward up to the ball of your foot. At the same time, make your final dribble just a little out to the side of your right foot. To keep the defender from swiping at the ball and knocking it away, make sure you make this dribble away from him. The dribble must be a strong one so the ball can bounce high to your hands (Fig. 6-11).

Also, as you make your last dribble, bend down in a crouched position and then spring upward. The actual mechanics of shooting the ball off the dribble will now be the same as if you were taking a stationary jump shot.

The Free Throw

WITH KYLE MACY
GUARD;   6'3",   195 LB.

Macy was the NBA's best free-throw shooter in the 1981–82 season (.889) and is the Phoenix Suns all-time leader from the free-throw line with an .890 percentage. An academic All-American as well as a basketball All-American at the University of Kentucky in 1980, Macy holds Kentucky's record for consecutive free throws with 32.

6-12a. Free-throw shooting is mainly concentration and rhythm. Here, Larry Bird sets himself at the line. His knees are slightly flexed, elbows bent, eyes on the rim.

Seventy percent of free-throw shooting is mental concentration. When you are at the free-throw line there is a lot of pressure on you. You have to think positively and tell yourself that you won't miss the shot. This confidence in your free-throw ability will come only from practice (Fig. 6-12*a,b,c*).

When I take my free throw I use the same shooting mechanics as I do when I take my jump shot. On the free-throw line I always start my routine by drying my hands on my socks. I then make sure that my feet are shoulders'-width apart, the heels parallel to each other. Some players like to stand with one foot in front of the other so the shooting hand is closer to the basket. In the end, however, you can't be influenced by how other players shoot their free throws, but you have to choose a shooting style that is most comfortable for you.

In addition to drying my hands, my routine also includes dribbling the ball three

6-12*b*. He raises his shooting arm, straightens his knees and prepares to release the ball.

times. This helps me to get into a good shooting rhythm. I follow this up by taking a couple of deep breaths and concentrating on the rim. At this point, the ball is held near my chest and my fingers are resting on the seams of the ball. I never rush my shot. When I finally feel ready to shoot, I use the same mechanics that I do with my jump shot, making sure that the shot is one continuous fluid motion.

In college I used to take between 25 and 50 free throws a day before practice. Now I practice the shot very little because I feel that I have already acquired the two secrets of successful free-throw shooting: concentration and proper shooting mechanics. When I do feel that I need to work on the shot, I'll just shoot enough in practice until I finally feel that I have the proper rhythm and concentration back once again.

6-12c. By snapping the wrist of his shooting arm and aiming his fingers at the rim, he ensures a full follow-through for his shot.

The Hook Shot

WITH KAREEM ABDUL-JABBAR
CENTER;   7'2",   240 LB.

Jabbar is the only NBA player to play for 17 seasons. He was selected to play in the All-Star game 16 times and has won six NBA MVP awards. Jabbar has scored 40 or more points 67 times in his career and ranks very high in virtually every statistical department in the NBA regular season and playoff records. Jabbar is a career 26.6-ppg scorer with many of his points coming from his unstoppable "sky hook."

6-13. The sky-hook of Kareem Abdul-Jabbar is nearly impossible to stop.

The hook is a soft and accurate shot, an excellent low-post move that all players should have in their offensive arsenal. When executed correctly, it's nearly impossible to block, even when guarded by a taller opponent (Fig. 6-13).

The hook shot always starts with your back to the basket. A good hook shot, like a good jump shot, depends on body balance. If you're not properly balanced during any part of the shot, your shot probably won't go in. Therefore, when you practice the hook, concentrate on form.

I like to catch the ball down low about 10 feet or closer to the hoop. Keep your legs

6-14*a,b,c,d.* **Kareem Abdul-Jabbar exhibits perfect form as he moves across the lane to shoot a right-handed hook shot against LaSalle Thompson. Note how he has moved into position to follow up his shot.**

flexed, your feet shoulders'-width apart or more. After receiving the ball, hold it at chest level with two hands. Flare your elbows out and hunch your shoulders slightly. To throw off your defender, you can fake first in the opposite direction. To make a right-hand hook shot, pivot on your rear foot (right) and take a long step into the lane with your left leg. The left foot should be turned toward the basket. Land with the heel of the left foot, roll forward off it and go up on the ball of your foot. Then rotate your body and begin to lift your right knee straight up (Fig. 6-14a,b,c,d).

As your knee begins to come up, the ball is lifted with both hands up past the side

of the head. The balance arm (left) is used to cradle the ball, but more importantly to protect it against defensive shot blockers. The shooting hand is raised upward, not too far from the body, with your wrist cocked outward. Release your balance hand from the ball before reaching maximum arm extension, and with your shooting hand, loft the ball toward the rim with a flick of your wrist. Put some backspin on the ball with your fingertips as the ball rolls off. The palm of your shooting hand should be nearly parallel with the floor as you follow through with the shot. The left arm is held outside to protect the shot. Try to land on the floor with both feet pointed toward the basket so you can immediately go in for a possible rebound and follow-up shot.

The Jump Hook

WITH BILL WALTON

The jump hook is an effective inside move for a big man caught down low. The move entails some body contact, but it will often result in a three-point play.

6-15a,b. Bill Walton scores many of his points inside the paint with a strong jump hook. When making the shot it's important to fend off your defender with your helper arm to keep him from getting to the ball.

The advantage of the jump hook over the regular hook shot is that it's much harder for a defender to lean against you and push you away from the basket. Since you are starting with a much lower center of gravity on the jump hook by simultaneously jumping up with both legs, the jump hook is a much more physically powerful move than the regular hook shot (Fig. 6-15a,b).

To make a jump hook with your right hand, start with your back to the basket. Pivot on your left foot and take a half step with your right leg. The defender's chest should now be at your shoulder and you are standing sideways to him. Bring the ball up

with two hands to face level and then jump up. Your left elbow is planted in the chest of the defender and this will keep him from getting to the ball. Cock your wrist on your shooting hand and release the ball at the height of your arm extension by flicking your wrist. After you shoot, go in for a possible rebound and second shot (Fig. 6-16).

6-16. Patrick Ewing goes high with this jump hook, fully extending his shooting arm while protecting the ball with his well-placed arm in the chest of his defender.

The Tap-In

WITH BUCK WILLIAMS

The tap-in is not really a shot per se. This move consists of only a soft flick of your fingertips. The fingertips are positioned under the ball as it comes off the rim and the ball is gently pushed up and tapped in the direction of the rim or backboard. Timing and good jumping ability are needed to perform this shot (Fig. 6-17).

6-17. Charles Barkley goes high for this tap over three players.

The Dunk

WITH DOMINIQUE WILKINS
FORWARD;   6'9",   215 LB.

An All-American at the University of Georgia, Wilkins left college for the NBA after his junior year in 1982 as the all-time leading scorer at Georgia. Nicknamed ''The Human Highlight Film'' for his spectacular dunks and incredible offensive wizardry, in just three seasons Wilkins moved himself up among the Atlanta Hawks all-time top ten in scoring average, offensive rebounds, blocked shots, and steals. He won the NBA slam dunk championship in 1985.

6-18a,b,c. Dominique Wilkins, one of the top leapers in pro basketball, executes the dunk, the game's most spectacular offensive move.

The dunk shot is one that can boost your teammates' spirits and quickly demoralize the opponent. Although the shot is spectacular and appears to be unrehearsed, it actually isn't. Your practice sessions and scrimmages are the time to be creative with the different dunks. This way you will have a good idea of what you can and cannot do in an actual game situation (Fig. 6-18a,b,c).

The Dunk II

WITH ORLANDO WOOLRIDGE
FORWARD;   6'9",   215 LB.

Woolridge has competed in the NBA slam dunk contest two times, losing out to Dominique Wilkins in 1985. A 16.5-ppg scorer, Woolridge began working on his dunk shots at Notre Dame, where he had a four-year field-goal percentage of .590. He currently is second best in the history of the Chicago Bulls for field-goal accuracy with a .545 mark.

Once I made dunking part of my offensive game in college I began to go to the basket a lot more aggressively. There is a time to dunk and a time not to throw it down.

6-19. Orlando Woolridge will go for a dunk shot whenever he has the space and can get his steps down.

6-20. At 7'4" Ralph Sampson towers over his opposition, making shots like this very difficult and dangerous to stop.

You have to know your strengths and limitations. Don't go for a dunk when you're out of position or you feel uncomfortable. Try for another shot in cases like this. But by all means, if you see that you do have the space and you can get your steps down, go for it (Fig. 6-19, 20, 21).

6-21a,b. Spud Webb, the 5'7", 140 lb. "little man" of the NBA, surprised everyone but himself when he beat seven challengers in the dunk con-test at the 1986 All-Star game. Webb dazzled the audience with an array of dunks which included 360s and bounces off the floor and backboard.

Shooting Drills

WITH KIKI VANDEWEGHE

When performing the following shooting drills, remember to concentrate on proper shooting form. By working regularly on these drills, you can add interest and fun to your daily workout.

1. Mark five to eight shooting spots on the floor at different distances from the basket. Start shooting jump shots first at the spot closest to the hoop, continuing until you make 10 baskets. Work your way around the court, repeating the drill at each of the spots that you marked on the floor.

2. While standing near the foul line, throw the ball out to the side a short distance from yourself. Chase after it, and then either drive in to the basket for a lay-up or else go straight up for a jump shot. Perform this drill on both sides of the court. This is an especially helpful drill because it recreates actual game situations where you get the ball on the run. The repetition that it offers will soon help make the various shots that you take on the move seem almost second nature to you.

CHAPTER 7

HOW TO RECEIVE THE BALL; SCREENS

The Chess Game

WITH JIM PAXSON

Go to any basketball game and your eyes will most likely follow the man with the ball and the player guarding him as they move about on the floor. A more careful observer, however, will be watching the offensive patterns as they develop within the team. It's these key offensive movements by the other four players as they set screens and move into position that will start a carefully orchestrated play, that, once set into motion and executed properly, will result in getting a player free for a shot.

Offensive basketball at its highest level is like a chess game. Players are strategically moved around the court without the ball in an effort to attack and exploit the defenses' weakest link. Most spectators don't realize the fact that a good portion of offensive basketball is actually played with the offensive players barely touching the basketball. In a 48-minute pro game, it's estimated that each starting player will have the ball in their hands for a total of only five minutes. A college player in a 40-minute game can expect to have the ball for only four minutes. A high school player in a full 32-minute game will barely have the ball in his possession for three minutes.

Work on the basic moves without the ball so they become well-used ingredients in your offensive repertoire. Remember, the more ways you know of to beat the defense, the easier it will be for you to get free for a shot.

BASIC MOVES WITHOUT THE BALL

The V-Step

WITH JIM PAXSON

A good defensive player will always do his best to keep you from getting the ball by positioning himself between you and the player with the ball. However, with the V-step move, an in and out, change-of-direction move, you can shake loose of your defender most anywhere on the court.

When your teammate has the ball on your side of the court and can't get it to you because you are being closely guarded, start to angle yourself down to the basket at three-fourths speed. Try to get close to the basket and to your defensive man. By being close to the man guarding you, you will actually have a better chance to free yourself from him once you sprint away.

When you're ready to cut back up for the ball, make body contact with your man and then sprint back up-court at a different angle. To do this, take a step with your inside foot (the one nearest the baseline), placing it near the lead foot of your defender. Put the weight of your body on your forward foot and push off. Sprint back up at a different angle and ask for the ball, making a target with your hand to receive a pass. Finally, with the ball in your hand, pivot around and square up to the basket. You are now ready to pass, shoot, or drive to the basket.

Reverse to the Ball

WITH JIM PAXSON

This is a move used to break free of your defensive man and then receive a pass. Begin by taking a step toward the forward foot of the defender with your leg that is nearer to the ball. Quickly make a 180-degree reverse toward the ball. While reversing, swing your outside leg in front of the defender, placing your arm on his outstretched arm to keep him from moving in and stealing or knocking away the incoming pass.

When you have the ball in your hand you can take a step forward with your foot nearest to the basket, turn, and face the hoop. Protect the ball.

Pop Out

WITH CLYDE DREXLER
FORWARD;   6'7",   210 LB.

A first-round draft choice from the University of Houston in 1983, Drexler's NBA career scoring high is 37 points. In the 1984–85 season Drexler averaged 17.2 ppg and led the Portland Trail Blazers with 73 double-figure scoring games.

7-1. Clyde Drexler makes contact with the chest of his defender and is ready to pop out quickly to the corner to receive a pass.

Here's a two-part move to get free of your defensive man and get the ball in your shooting range. To make the move, go at three-fourths speed down toward the basket. Once you get in a position where you are just behind your man's head and he has to turn to look for you, take a final hard step, make contact with the chest of your defensive man with your forearm to freeze him there for an instant, then "pop out" at full speed, moving away from the basket to the side-court. Present your shooting hand as a target to the passer (Fig. 7-1).

The Back Door

WITH JIM PAXSON

The back-door play is another very effective change-of-direction move to be used when your defensive man is overplaying you, blocking your receiving lane, or otherwise preventing you from receiving a pass.

7-2a,b. Jim Paxson leads his defender in one direction with his left arm and leg, but then quickly pivots and cuts back-door to receive a pass as he heads toward the hoop.

To go back-door—cut behind your defender when you are overplayed—you need coordination between you and the passer. Signal him with your eyes or with a wave of the hand. If you have been playing regularly together he'll know immediately from the defensive setup what you want to do (and vice versa) and no signal will be needed. First, lure your defender away from the hoop by taking two steps at three-fourths speed toward the passer. Then, changing pace, take a quick, hard step with your outside foot, pivot, and take a long first step with your inside foot at full speed, cutting to the basket. With your defender now behind you, ask for the ball, make a target with your outside hand, catch the pass, and go in for your shot (Figs. 7-2a,b).

You can also make a back door by using a reverse move. Start by taking two steps toward the ball. On your second step put your inside foot (the foot nearer the baseline) next to the back foot of your defender, and make a 270-degree reverse. Use your hand and inside arm and place it on the defender's hip or back. This will "hold" him a split second in his position and give you a chance to safely break for the basket to receive the pass.

The Front Cut

WITH JIM PAXSON

This cut is used when you are playing high and want to receive the ball going toward the basket. Your defender is facing you, standing between you and the basket, and this makes it difficult to penetrate. To get around this, move at moderate speed toward the defender. Getting close to him is essential if this move is to work. Once you do get near him, make a hard step with your outside foot, then a crossover step in front of him with your inside foot. Cut to the basket to receive a pass.

Fake Screen and Cut

WITH JIM PAXSON

To execute this move, you simply go away from the ball and set a fake screen. But instead of making the screen, you then make a 180-degree turn by pivoting on your inside foot to receive the pass.

Another option is to make a change-of-direction after the fake screen and then cut to the basket to receive a pass.

The Screen

WITH JEFF RULAND
CENTER;   6'11",   275 LB.

Ruland, an 18.6 ppg scorer, played basketball for one season in Spain before joining the Bullets for the 1981–82 season. He made the All-Rookie team that year, while leading the Bullets in rebounding and field-goal percentage. His career one-game scoring high is 38 points and his one-game rebound high is 24.

A screen, also called a pick, is a legal block set by an offensive player on the side of or behind a defender in order to free a teammate to take a shot or receive a pass.

You have to be prepared to take a lot of physical pounding when you set a screen. That's just the nature of screening. Another human body will soon be slamming into you—probably while running at close to full speed.

When I set a screen I always first set a good base for myself by spreading my feet wide and bending my knees slightly. This way, when the defensive player smashes into me, he'll bounce off and I'll still be standing. My arms are kept at my sides. Another way to protect yourself is to hold your fists tightly over the opposite wrists, keeping your arms extended downward.

You can screen for a teammate anytime and anywhere on the court, but screening properly takes a bit of teamwork in order to work correctly. Once you've played the game for a while and know how to screen, you'll start to do it naturally. When you see that a teammate is in trouble you'll automatically go and set a screen for him.

A good screen is all a matter of angles and timing. It should be set perpendicular to the direction that the defense expects to move and the screener must use the hip of the defensive player to be screened as his target.

The moment it's understood that you will set a screen, the teammate you'll be screening for will have to do his part by setting his defensive man up properly. This means that he'll first take him at moderate speed a few steps away from the screen. This relaxes the defender somewhat. Then, boom! Your teammate will use a change of pace and change of direction and run or dribble quickly very close off your shoulder.

It's important that your teammate comes close to you on the screen. If he makes the mistake of going a step or two away from you, the screen will lose most of its effectiveness, especially when a good defensive man is guarding him. Just a foot of space is all that's needed for the defense to slide in between you and your teammate and pick him up again.

After you set a screen, make a 180-degree turn and look to receive a possible pass. You'll be surprised to find how many times you are free after setting a screen.

The Different Types of Screens

WITH JEFF RULAND

There are four different types of screens:

- A *vertical* screen is set down low (Fig. 7-3). Run your man either up or down off the screen to break free.

- A *horizontal* screen is made over the top or else parallel to the sideline (Figs. 7-4a,b).

- A *diagonal* screen is usually set in the three-second area. The screener goes from one upper corner to the opposite low corner of the lane or vice-versa.

- A *blind* screen (a "back pick") is usually made behind the back of the defensive man. You can make the screen either with your chest or with your rear end (Fig. 7-5).

7-3. Sidney Moncrief runs his man off this well-made Terry Cummings vertical screen and moves out to receive an incoming pass.

7-4a,b. Larry Bird fakes a pass into Kevin McHale and then uses his horizontal screen to lose his man and go in for a drive.

7-5. Bernard King braces himself as players crash into him while he sets a blind screen for Darrell Walker.

How to Use the Screen

WITH ALEX ENGLISH
FORWARD;   6'7", 190 LB.

English had a career high of 47 points for the Denver Nuggets in a triple-overtime loss to Detroit in the 1982–83 season, the same year that he won the NBA scoring title (28.4 ppg). He exploded in the 1985–86 season with a 54-point game against Houston. English has a nine-year pro 20.4-ppg regular-season average and a 24.4-ppg playoff average. He has played in five All-Star games.

7-6. Kiki Vandeweghe pushes off the screen of Kenny Carr and starts to fade back toward the sideline for an incoming pass.

The effectiveness of the screen depends not only on the screener, but also on the player who receives the screen. This player must be able to read the defense and react accordingly without predetermining which way he will go. It is the defensive alignment which actually dictates this.

There are four basic ways to take advantage of a screen:

- The *front cut*. If your defender is properly screened, make a front cut over the top of the screen.

- The *back door*. If the defensive man tries to slide over the top of the screen, make a fake to go over the top of the screen with your outside foot and then quickly change your direction and cut down to the basket.

- The *pop out*. If your defender drops off or tries to go between you and the screener, pop out to receive the ball. To signal this play to the screener, push him on his hip. As he feels you moving away from him, he will know that he should then cut to the basket to receive the pass from you.

- The *fade*. If your defensive man is making it difficult for you to use the screen by playing you high on the top side or toward the middle, move quickly toward the screen, push the screener on his hip, and then drop back toward the baseline (Fig. 7-6).

CHAPTER

8

ONE-ON-ONE OUTSIDE MOVES WITH THE BALL

The Excitement of Basketball

WITH MICHAEL JORDAN

GUARD; 6'6", 200 LB.

In the 1984–85 season Michael Jordan finished his rookie season in fine fashion by leading the Chicago Bulls in almost every statistical category. He played 38.3 minutes a game, grabbed 6.5 rpg, had 5.9 assists, 2.39 steals a game, and averaged 28.2 ppg, the third best in the NBA. He was the only player in the NBA to score in double figures in all 82 games played. Jordan, selected Rookie of the Year, led the Bulls in scoring in 57 games and had a high of 49 against Detroit. In an injury-plagued 1985–86 season, Jordan had a career-high 63 points in a playoff game against Boston.

Many times you'll receive a pass on the court and find that, although you are guarded, you are the closest one to the basket. It's now up to you to make a move with the ball so you can get your shot off. This is where you get to add your personal offensive touch and is what makes the game so exciting to play. Being able to execute more than one of the following individual moves with the ball will greatly help you to get free for your shot. Practice them when you're alone, using different fakes and speed variations.

When you practice these moves, be sure that you turn and face the basket and assume proper basketball position: your feet are shoulders'-width apart and pointed toward the basket; your knees are flexed; your shoulders are facing the basket. Also, hold the ball securely with two hands close to your body. If you are right-handed, keep the ball on your right side; if you are left-handed, keep it on the left side.

LIVE-BALL MOVES

The Drive

WITH SIDNEY MONCRIEF
GUARD;   6'4",   185 LB.

Sidney Moncrief averaged 20.2 ppg in the 1985–86 season. An All-American, and the leading scorer and rebounder in University of Arkansas history, Moncrief is a six-time NBA All-Star selection.

The drive, a quick move past the defender toward the hoop, is one of the most basic of all offensive basketball moves. If you are able to drive well, then you can get past your man and successfully penetrate the defense. Once you are close to the hoop you can then go in for a shot yourself, possibly getting fouled as you're going for the shot. Or you can pass off to a teammate who can get an uncontested lay-up or short-range jump shot.

Don't overuse the drive. What happens in a game when you continually look for the drive is that your defensive man automatically starts to back up once you have the ball in your possession. He knows what you want to do, so by backing up he denies you the first step to the hoop. This takes away any advantage that you had over him with the drive.

When this happens, a player has to bring out the best offensive weapon there is to get the drive back: the outside shot. If the defense is laying off you to keep you from driving, then go up for your jumper. After you make two or three of them, the defense will be forced to move back in close to keep you honest. Then you've got your man just where you want him. He's more vulnerable than ever to your quickness, and you can use your drive once again.

When I receive the ball I can set my man up for a drive by using a ball, shoulder, or head fake. Depending on the position of my defender I can also fake a jump shot, get my man in the air, and go around him.

When my man does go for one of my fakes, I push off on my pivot foot, take a long, quick first step toward the hoop, and put the ball down hard on the floor (so it bounces back quickly to my hand) just past the hip of the defender. When the ball is put down, I lift my pivot foot, push past the defender's shoulder, and go to the hoop. It's important when you're driving to protect the ball with your body, turning your trunk as much as possible to prevent any possible steals.

For a drive to the basket, quickness and control are great assets to have. To practice your drive, assume the basketball position, keeping low for more quickness. With the ball in your hands, work on pushing off on your back foot and taking that first long step to the hoop. Once this first quick step starts to come naturally, you're on your way to becoming a dangerous driver (Fig. 8-1).

8-1. Sidney Moncrief has one of the quickest first steps in basketball. Here he goes one-on-one with Rory Sparrow as he prepares to drive to the hoop.

When you do commit yourself to going up for the shot after your drive, concentrate on making the shot. It's going to be congested as you move to the hoop, and other players will pop out to pick you up. Concentrate on making your shot. Look to pass only if you can't get your shot off or if you spot a teammate in better scoring position.

8-2. Michael Jordan jabs with his right foot to test the reaction of his defender. He can now go up for a jump shot or drive around his man to the hoop.

The Jab Step

WITH MICHAEL JORDAN

The jab step is a common foot fake which, depending on the defensive player's reaction, is used to set up either a drive or a jump shot.

To perform a jab step, keep the ball in your hands at waist level or near your hips and establish proper basketball position. Take a short, hard step (10 inches or less) toward your defensive man while at the same time faking the dribble by bringing the ball down outside your knee when you make the jab with your foot. Pause slightly to see the reaction of the defensive player (Fig. 8-2).

Depending on what your defender does after you've moved toward him, you now make the next move quickly. If the defender lunges toward you, then take a longer step with the same foot and simultaneously push the ball out and drive right around his hip. To get this move down in your mind, think of it as a one-two count move with a split second stop in the middle (Fig. 8-3a, b).

When you make the jab-step move and your defensive player plays you for it—he backs up and blocks your path—your next offensive possibility would be to take a jump shot. You can do it by first pulling back your lead foot and then going up for the shot, or else by going up for the shot without bringing your lead foot back. Take the shot whichever way feels most comfortable for you.

It's important when you are going to make a jab step that your first step is not too long. Go out too far and you'll be off balance, unable to successfully make your drive or jump shot. Secondly, remember to keep in a crouched position with your knees bent. This coiled position assures you enough power to make the drive or jump shot.

The Rocker Step

WITH MICHAEL JORDAN

The rocker step is a quick head-and-shoulder fake you can use to set up a drive. It begins just like the jab step. Take a short hard step toward your defensive man and then fake a drive. Once you see he hasn't been fooled, pull back to your original position and, when your defensive man moves toward you again, drive past him leading with the same jab foot. Think of this as a three-count move: jab step; rock back to your original position; powerful step and strong dribble past the hip of your defensive man.

8-3a,b. Julius Erving uses his jab step against Larry Bird and then steps back and takes the jump shot when Bird blocks his path to the hoop.

Rocker Step, Shot Fake, and Drive

WITH JULIUS ERVING
FORWARD;   6'6",   210 LB.

Julius Erving is the number-three all-time scorer in NBA history behind Wilt Chamberlain and Kareem Abdul-Jabbar. For 14 straight years as a pro player, first in the ABA and then in the NBA, he has averaged 20 ppg or better. Erving has also played in ten consecutive NBA All-Star games.

Start this move by taking a jab step and then rocking back. Fake a jump shot with your arms and ball by bringing the ball up to the level of your head as you would in the

8-4a,b. Andrew Toney crouches low and uses the crossover step to get around his man. Note how he uses his helper hand to fend off the arm of the defender as he moves to the hoop.

first phase of a jump shot. Once your defender is taken in by your fake and moves toward you to block your jump shot, make an explosive drive and go right around him.

As with all of these individual moves, it's important to maintain a crouched position when you make your fakes and when you go around your defender. If you straighten up, you'll lose the power and quickness which makes these moves so effective.

The Crossover Step

WITH JULIUS ERVING

Often the defensive player will overplay you to your strong side, that side of the court he feels you will always move toward in order to get your shot off. This strategy, he hopes, will prevent you from making any good offensive moves in that direction. However, the crossover step and the ability to dribble equally well with either hand will help you out of this defensive overplay (Fig. 8-4a,b).

To make the crossover step to your left side, first make a short, hard jab step in the direction of the defensive player with your right foot. Then, keep low and with the *same* leg take a long step, crossing it over to the outside of the defender's right foot. Swing the ball very quickly from your right side to your left side as you make the leg move, cutting closely off the defender's shoulder. Push the ball out behind the defender with your left hand, making sure it goes past his hip.

DEAD-BALL MOVES

The Shot Fake and Jump Shot

WITH ADRIAN DANTLEY
FORWARD/GUARD;   6'5",   210 LB.

Dantley is the Utah Jazz career leader in points, scoring average, minutes, field goals, field-goal attempts, and free throws. The 1977 Rookie of the Year from Notre Dame has never shot less than 51 percent for a season and only three times has shot less than 80 percent from the free-throw line. A 26.1-ppg career scorer, Dantley had four consecutive 30-ppg seasons between 1980 and 1984.

Many times you will encounter situations in a game when you have already picked up your dribble and your defensive man is standing right in front of you preventing you from getting off a shot or passing the ball. It is just for cases like this that you need to have some dead-ball moves in your repertoire. Naturally, you can use these moves away from the basket, but they are most effective when you make them not far from the hoop, either in or close to the lane.

To make the shot fake and jump shot move, start with a one-count stop. Bring the ball up toward your head to give the defensive man the impression that you are going to take a jump shot. He will lunge toward you at this moment. As he moves in, crouch down with your legs to gather your strength and then go up for the jump shot just as your defensive man moves into you. Go up strong and bump him a little with your shoulder or forearm to keep him from blocking your shot. Often your man will foul you and you can get a three-point play out of the move (Fig. 8-5).

**8-5. Adrian Dantley bump-fakes his two Rocket
defenders, hoping to get them to foul him when
he finally goes to the basket.**

Crossover

WITH ADRIAN DANTLEY

This is another power move that will help get you past your defender after you've given up your dribble. It basically entails making a one-count stop, making a crossover step and then going past your defender to shoot a lay-up. Since this is a power move, making the shot will depend a lot on getting jumping power and positioning from your lower body. Be prepared to be fouled as you go to the hoop. Protect the ball from your man with your elbow as you go up.

Step-Through Move

WITH MARK AGUIRRE
FORWARD;   6'6",   232 LB.

Aguirre is the Dallas Mavericks' all-time leader in points. He has 15 of the Mavs' 18 regular-season 40-plus scoring games, four 45-plus games, and has Dallas's only ''triple double'' with 20 points, 11 rebounds, and 16 assists in a 1983 game against Denver.

After a one-count stop, fake a jump shot. If you want to go to the left, take a quick step to the side of the defender with your right foot and protect the ball as you go toward the hoop. Remember to stay low; this will give power to your move. When you go to the hoop, don't make your steps too long. This will cause you to lose both power and speed.

ONE-ON-ONE INSIDE MOVES WITHOUT AND WITH THE BALL

Where the Games Are Won

WITH KAREEM ABDUL-JABBAR

It's a necessity in winning basketball that a team have players with good, solid inside moves. These are the players (and not only the centers) who can post up their man, receive a pass inside the lane or down low "in traffic," and then turn it into a high-percentage shot and a possible three-point play. The more players a team has like this, the better off it will be, because a team that can rely on good inside movement for many of its points has these positive factors working in its favor:

• It can count on getting most of its points from shots taken only a few feet away from the hoop instead of having to depend on long-range jump shots.

145

- Three-point plays, a field goal and foul shot, are more likely to occur "in the paint" than on shots taken from outside.

- Strong, continuous offensive play underneath the basket and the resulting personal fouls committed by the defense will quickly change the complexion of any game.

- A player with good inside moves will cause the defense to double up and help out to keep him from scoring. This defensive maneuvering often results in freeing offensive forwards and guards for their outside jump shots.

Make Yourself Bigger

WITH BILL WALTON

To play down low you have to make yourself bigger. You do this by setting yourself up with an exaggerated basketball stance. Spread your feet out wider than shoulders' width. Make sure that your elbows are flared and that your hands are up. What this big stance does for you is help keep your defensive man from stepping around you or reaching over your back to either steal or knock the ball away.

When fighting for position down low, the most important thing to do is to present yourself as a good target for your teammates to pass to. With so many players cutting in and out of the low-post area, this is often very difficult. Your own defender will be doing his best to get in front of you and cut off any passes, and any other defender coming through the low-post area will throw out his hand if it looks like he can steal an incoming pass (Fig. 9-1).

Keep your man behind you at all times by continually maneuvering in front of him, blocking him with your upper arm, while at the same time presenting a target for a pass with your other arm held up high. It's extremely important to have contact with the body of your defender so you can always know where he is and what type of move you can then try to make. To work successfully in the low post or in the lane, it will take a coordinated effort between the passer and you to finally get you the ball.

9-1. Bill Walton presents himself as an imposing target as he fronts Buck Williams and calls for the ball.

HOW TO RECEIVE THE BALL: DEFENDER ON THE SIDE OR BEHIND

The Rear Turn

WITH ALVAN ADAMS
CENTER; 6'9", 218 LB.

Adams is the Phoenix Suns all-time leader in rebounds, assists, steals, blocked shots, games played, and scoring. NBA Rookie of the Year in 1976, Adams has a 15.4-ppg career scoring average with one-game career highs of 47 points and 19 rebounds.

When you're being closely guarded from behind in the low post, you often need to make a quick rear turn to spring yourself free to receive a pass. This move is made by hooking your outside foot around the outside foot of your defensive man and then quickly pivoting on your lead foot. Bend over slightly as you make the turn, being sure to make contact with your man with your rear and back.

Once you have good positioning, ask for the ball with either one or two hands. Hold this position for a few seconds so the player with the ball can see you (Fig. 9-2a,b).

To prevent your defensive man from interfering with the incoming pass, it's important that you seal him off by putting the forearm of your "non-target" arm, bent at a 45-degree angle, on his chest, without using the hand to push or hold him.

Another effective way of keeping the defender from reaching over and stealing a pass is to hook your non-target forearm in the crook of the defender's extended arm and push it down. Continue to signal for the ball with your other arm.

The Step Across

WITH ALVAN ADAMS

When your defender is playing in front of you on the ball side in the low post you will never be able to receive a good pass unless you can get back in front of your man.

The best way to do this is to make a strong step in the direction away from the ball and then come back quickly. Step in front of your defender with the foot nearest the ball. By keeping low and leaning against the leg and hip of your man, you will seal him off and keep him from getting around you again. Put your arm up and call for the ball (Fig. 9-3*a*,*b*,*c*,*d*).

9-2*a*,*b*. Kareem Abdul-Jabbar executes a rear turn to break free of Mark Eaton's defense and set up to receive a low-post pass.

9-3*a,b,c,d.* Larry Bird is fronted by Magic Johnson and quickly executes a step-across move to
receive the ball in the low post.

The Reverse

WITH JACK SIKMA

CENTER;   6'11",   250 LB.

Jack Sikma was Seattle's first-round draft choice in 1977 and was named to the NBA All-Rookie team the following year after averaging 10.7 ppg and 8.2 rpg. Sikma's rugged play under the boards helped lead Seattle to the NBA championship in 1979.

If you are positioned down low on the ball side but your man is keeping you from getting a pass, a good way to get the ball is with a reverse. This move entails circling around your man, checking him in his place, and then getting the pass.

To make the reverse work for you, take a hard step toward the passer and then make a drop step with your foot nearest to the baseline. Hook the defender's back foot with your foot and lean into his hip with your hip and forearm. This will hold him in his spot and keep him from going around you. With your free hand call for the ball and be ready to go right up to the hoop with it.

HOW TO RECEIVE THE BALL: DEFENDER IN FRONT

The Lob Pass

WITH ADRIAN DANTLEY

Timing between you and the passer is critical if this play is going to work. The pass has to be accurate and out of reach of the defender's hands, and you have to effectively hold off your defender before breaking from him to receive the pass and take it to the hoop.

The lob pass is best used when your man is fronting you down low on the ball side. When this happens, turn and face the basket and lean your hip and buttocks into the back of your defender. Place your forearm on his back and with your other hand make a

9-4. Bernard King holds off Mike O'Koren with one hand and calls for a lob pass to the hoop with his shooting hand. Timing between passer and receiver is critical in the congested area under the hoop.

target for the incoming lob pass. Once the pass is over the hands of your defender and near you, release from the defender, take the pass, and go up to the hoop with it (Fig. 9-4).

Ball Reversal

WITH MOSES MALONE

Many times your man will do a good job of fronting you and keeping you from getting a pass down low. When this happens on the ball side, what you can do is signal to your teammate to swing the ball over to the opposite side of the court. As this is happening, turn your back on your defender and lean into him, effectively holding him in his position. Once the ball has come to the other side you now are at a much better angle to receive an incoming pass and your defender is now behind you, unable to pick off the pass.

The Flash Cut

WITH JULIUS ERVING

The flash cut is always made from the "help side," the side away from the ball, and entails moving toward the passer from either the low- or high-post area. To make a flash cut you have to first take a step or two away from where you want to go. This helps throw off your defensive man. Then change your direction, pick up your pace, and cut toward the passer to receive the ball. Your defender will be behind you at this point and you can either go up for a shot or pass off.

HOW TO GO TO THE BASKET

Drop Step to the Baseline and Power Move

WITH TERRY CUMMINGS
FORWARD; 6'9",   235 LB.

Cummings was Rookie of the Year in the 1982–83 season, a year in which he ranked 10th in the League in both scoring (23.7 ppg) and rebounding (10.6 rpg). Cummings has scored 20 or more points more than 200 times in his NBA career. His regular-season scoring and rebounding highs are 39 points and 24 rebounds.

The drop step is one of the most important weapons any low-post player can have. It should be your first option when you're down low with your back to the basket.

Once you have received the ball and your defender is playing behind you, give a shoulder-and-ball fake towards the lane and follow it up by dropping and then hooking your inside foot (the foot nearest the baseline) around the foot of your defender. Make a 270-degree turn, keeping your knees bent as you turn. Explode to the basket with both arms going up with the ball. Use your non-shooting arm to protect the ball from the defender (Figs. 9-5*a,b*).

This move can also be made using a dribble. In this case, once you make your turn, take a strong dribble with your inside hand (the one nearest the baseline), protecting the ball with your body (Figs. 9-6*a,b*).

Drop Step and Reverse

WITH TERRY CUMMINGS

If your defender reacts properly to the drop step and is able to block your path along the baseline (or in the middle), you can pivot and make a reverse in the opposite direction, ending the move with a power shot, a jump hook, or a lay-up.

Drop Step to the Middle and Hook

WITH KEVIN McHALE
FORWARD;   6'10",   225 LB.

McHale was named to the All-Rookie team in 1981, the same year his Boston Celtic team won the NBA championship. McHale averaged 21.3 ppg in the 1985–86 season and won the 1985 NBA Sixth Man Award for his play coming off the bench. McHale played in the 1984 and 1986 All-Star games.

The drop step to the middle and hook is a very good alternative for under-the-basket play when your path along the baseline is blocked. Start the move with a fake toward the baseline and then take a drop step with your outside foot (the foot farthest from the hoop) in the direction of the free-throw-lane area. As you move into the lane, keep the ball close to your body near your chin, protecting it with your shoulder and

9-5a,b. Robert Parish uses the drop step to get around Kareem Abdul-Jabbar.

9-6a,b. Kevin McHale prepares to receive the incoming pass and use the drop step toward the baseline against Bob McAdoo.

elbow from your defensive man (Fig. 9-7*a,b,c*). Depending on who is guarding you, you can now take either a regular hook shot or a jump hook. Once you shoot be ready to go in for a possible rebound.

9-7*a,b,c*. Kevin McHale uses his long first step to get position in the lane and protects the ball from his defender with his non-shooting arm as he goes up for a jump hook.

Drop Step to the Baseline, Turn, and Jump Hook

WITH KEVIN McHALE

Make a drop step to the baseline, keeping low and protecting the ball as you spin. If your defensive man has blocked your path, make a front turn, face the basket, and then go up for your jump shot. You can also make a similar move by starting with a drop step to the center, pivoting, facing the basket, and then taking a jump shot (Fig. 9-8*a,b,c*).

Drop Step, Turn, Jump Shot Fake, and Crossover

WITH MOSES MALONE

When the baseline is blocked by your man after you have made a drop step, turn and face the basket, pivoting on your outside foot (the foot furthest away from the

9-8*a,b,c.* Kevin McHale adds more dimension to his play under the basket with this drop step to the center, turn and jump shot.

baseline). Fake a jump shot by bringing the ball quickly up to head level. When your defender starts to approach you, bring the ball down, cross your non-pivot foot in front of the defender and go past him toward the hoop. You can either make a power move up to the basket or try a hook shot.

Turnaround Jump Shot

WITH RALPH SAMPSON
FORWARD;   7'4",   230 LB.

Sampson was the first college player selected in the 1983 college draft and he easily won Rookie of the Year honors playing for the Houston Rockets in the 1983–84 season. He was named MVP of the 1985 All-Star game following a 24-point, 10-rebound performance.

The turnaround jumper is a fundamental move that any player should have who plays with his back to the basket. To make this jump shot, pivot with either your inside or outside foot (Fig. 9-9a,b,c). Step away from your defender with your other foot as you are pivoting. This will give you adequate space to get your jump shot off without having it blocked. Once you have completely turned and are facing the basket, go up for your shot (Fig. 9-10).

Up, Turn, and Duck Under

WITH ARTIS GILMORE
CENTER;   7'2",   260 LB.

Gilmore ranks 12th on the NBA all-time scoring list with a 20.0-ppg career scoring average. His .580 career field-goal accuracy is an NBA record. Gilmore has played in six NBA All-Star games.

My bread-and-butter move under the basket is one that I first started to use in high school and later perfected in college. You make this move by posting up on the left side of the lane near the box. Once you have the ball, bring it up on your left side for a fake while at the same time making a drop step with your right foot into the lane. Bring the ball down and turn inside. Pump fake your opponent once. If you can't shoot immediately, then go up to the hoop for a lay-up or dunk. Be prepared to get fouled as you go in (Fig. 9-11a,b,c,d).

9-9a,b,c. Ralph Sampson works on his turn-around jump shot at a practice session. Note how he protects the ball with his hip as he quickly pivots to set up his shot.

9-10. Ralph Sampson shooting his turnaround jumper in traffic.

9-11*a,b,c,d.* **Artis Gilmore relies on finesse and strength around the basket to get his shots off against defenders. Here he practices his special up, turn, and duck under move that brings him so many of his points.**

The Step-Forward Jump Shot

WITH JACK SIKMA

This is a move I use very often because it lets me take advantage of my jump shot from close range. The movement starts with your back to the basket. Once you receive the ball, take a step forward and away from your defender with the ball held high. After you step away, make a rear turn and face the basket. Once you are completely facing the basket, go up for your jump shot (Fig. 9-12).

The Defense Dictates Your Shots

WITH MARK AGUIRRE

When you finally have the ball in your possession you should be very aware of the defensive pressure. By knowing exactly which players are around you, you'll know what shots you can take and also whom you can pass out to if need be.

9-12. Jack Sikma's step-back jump shot is very hard to defend against because it catches the defensive man by surprise.

9-13. Mark Aguirre uses his left hand to feel where his defensive man is while using his right arm to call for the ball. How his man plays him after he receives the ball will determine Aguirre's next move.

My basic thinking when I have the ball down low is that I don't have a precon-ceived notion of which shot I will take. Rather, I'll take whatever shot the defense will give me. I know which move I can make by feeling the body pressure that my man puts against me.

Only by determining how your defender is guarding you can you know which move you can make. Once you understand the defensive pressure for what it is on that particular play, you'll know which shot (or shots) is open for you (Fig. 9-13).

Many coaches refer to this concept as "reading the defense"; the player who can "read" in this manner knows what his defensive man is doing to him at all times, and knows how to react properly so he can receive a pass and get his shot off.

Being able to read the defense and counteract it with several different options will make you a very potent offensive threat as well as a candidate for many three-point plays.

Life Underneath

WITH ADRIAN DANTLEY

The real reason for my success down low comes from my high school coach. I had to play center for my high school team and therefore needed to learn how to pivot off both feet, plant myself, then make a power move to the hoop without traveling. My coach drilled me on these moves every day until I could finally do them right.

I'm surprised to see that most big men in the league today can't make effective moves underneath. I guess *the* reason for this is that they simply never were taught them. Or they never worked hard enough on them. Or if they did work on them, they learned the moves later on in their careers and haven't really been able to master them.

When I'm down low I move by instinct. I feel my man on my hip and when I can tell he's leaning or pushing more on one part of my body than the other, I'll keep low and try to go in the direction away from where he's leaning.

Even when I'm closely guarded I'm often able to turn, face up, and either shoot my jump shot or else go in for a power drive. However, there are some players who play me very tight, so that I can't get my jumper off so easily. What I have to do against them is shoot right after I turn around to the basket. If I delay or don't get the shot off quickly enough, either the shot will be blocked or else I'll be tied up and forced to pass out.

Playing underneath is tough, no question about it. You have to be willing to get fouled and take a beating. I prepare myself for this in the summer by playing with friends, working especially on my moves under the basket. We'll often play half-court for four or five baskets, and allow grabbing and holding when a player goes to the basket. Other times we'll decide to play the entire game without calling fouls. By playing like this, I'm able to concentrate on making my offensive move and following through with my shot even though I'm being pushed and shoved while I'm doing it. It often gets like that or even rougher when you play underneath in the NBA.

CHAPTER 10

BASKETBALL AND YOU: SACRIFICE, MOTIVATION, DESIRE

Mastery of basketball's fundamentals, and the translation of that mastery into success on the court, takes plenty of sacrifice, motivation, and desire. But even if you are starting out with limited or average athletic talent, or only play with friends in the evenings or at the park, there is still hope for you to become a better player. If you have the burning desire to put in the hours of practice that are required, you will soon begin to increase your abilities and gain confidence in yourself. Perhaps, after logging hundreds of hours of practice, you might even become an All-American basketball player.

Basketball pros have made it to the NBA with a little bit of luck, but basically they earned their spot on a roster through hard work, perseverance, and talent. No one ever starts out in the game of basketball as a superstar. One look at the biographies of NBA

All-Star players will tell you that. Every year the All-Star team is made up of players who had been cut from their high school team—some more than once. Others saw little playing time for some portion of their high school careers and only blossomed during college. Although many high school players give up under similar circumstances, these future pro players were different: they kept on practicing, redoubling their efforts to make the team and improve. It was their burning desire to excel in a game that they loved and not to give up until they achieved their dreams that eventually took them all the way to the NBA.

Basketball is not an easy game to master. To become an exceptional basketball player who stands out among the hundreds of thousands who play the game every year is nearly impossible. Each year less than 300 players make up active NBA rosters.

To become a player with a good grasp of basketball fundamentals isn't all that easy either. It means putting in long hours of practice, even when everyone around you may be shaking their heads and saying that you're wasting your time. But by working on the fundamentals and drills that have been outlined in this book, you will have at your fingertips the building blocks needed to make yourself a sound player.

Basketball is a social sport. It offers a great way to make new friends and satisfy your competitive urges at the same time. When compared to other team sports, basketball is at the top of the list for keeping you in top physical shape. You may not want more from the game than this.

However, some of you may have much higher ambitions: to be picked for your high school varsity team, to earn a college scholarship, to play basketball in Europe, or eventually to be one of the few chosen to play in the National Basketball Association. Whatever your personal goals might be, whether to score double figures, to hold your man below his scoring average, or to become the best rebounder or shot-blocker on your team, be realistic in your ambitions by making sure that you set *attainable* short- and long-term goals.

A short-term goal for a high school player could be just making the varsity by eleventh grade with hopes of scoring in double figures. A long-term goal would be being selected to the All-League team at the end of your senior year and being offered a college basketball scholarship.

Whatever your particular goals may be, sit down, think them through, and then write them down on a piece of paper. Over the next few weeks as you begin to achieve your short-term goals, sit down again and write new ones for yourself and work toward achieving them as well. Eventually, once your short- and long-term goals have been fulfilled in high school, new ones can be set as you move along to higher levels of organized basketball.

As you will come to see, your goals can't be attained unless you are willing to put the effort into practicing and playing. You have to be willing to make sacrifices with your time, be motivated to have consistently good workouts, and sustain your desire to achieve your goals. This entails doing something with your basketball every day of the year.

For most young players, it's during the summer months that the greatest progress with your game can be made. While friends have headed off to the beach for swimming and relaxation, you should be practicing on your own, using the drills and exercises in this book to shore up the weaker points of your game. Or else attending a basketball camp or clinic. Or playing in local summer leagues.

Basketball is not an easy sport to master, and you will face many roadblocks as you try to improve. At times you may even become discouraged and begin to question your ambitions. A successful athlete, however, won't let any obstacle deter him for long. And neither should you. If you want to be a winner, you won't quit until you achieve those goals you have set for yourself.

The more you become involved with basketball, the more you'll see that it will demand everything from you. But if you are willing to give everything in return, you just might eventually fulfill most, if not all, of your sports dreams. Once you have mastered the fundamentals, can consistently hit your shots, and can play tough defense from tip-off to the final buzzer, it's possible that the loftiest of all the basketball dreams, a career in the National Basketball Association, might one day become a reality for you. Good luck!

AUTHOR PROFILES

GIORGIO GANDOLFI is the leading European authority on American basketball. His feature articles about pro players and the NBA appear monthly in the Italian *Giganti del Basket* and the French *Maxi Basket* magazines. Gandolfi is the author of *The NBA Coaches Handbook* and five other books about basketball and football. He lives in Cremona, Italy, where he is the European representative of the National Basketball Coaches Association.

GERALD SECOR COUZENS played basketball in France for four years after graduating from Princeton University. He is the author of five other books about sports and fitness. In 1983 his company, SportsDreams, organized the first basketball camp for players over 30 years old to work out with and play against former NBA greats.